A WISDOM SERIES BOOK

Printed in the United States of America

Library of Congress Control Number: 2021906253
First Printing, 2021

ISBN: 978-0-9987925-9-0

Lights On Publishing
Tucson, AZ

PATHWAYS TO WISDOM

—

What We Learn Makes Us Smart, What We Do Makes Us Wise

By Jim Schell

LIGHTS ON PUBLISHING

TUCSON, AZ

Also by JIM SCHELL

The Brass Tacks Entrepreneur
Small Business Management Guide
Small Business Answer Book
Small Business for Dummies (co-author)
How to Use Your Financial Statements to Manage Your Business
What Makes Bend Special
The Magic of Mentoring
So, You Want to Be an Entrepreneur. Read This Book First.
How to Make Your Community's Economy Sizzle
How to Recharge Your Nonprofit's Board of Directors
Peer-to-Peer Groups. Learning from Those You Trust
Why Retirement Sucks
Where Wisdom Comes From

To Maisie, the best editor. Ever. You make words work.

CONTENTS

PART TWO: THE WISDOM WE LEARN FROM PEOPLE

PART THREE: THE WISDOM WE LEARN FROM THE WORLD AROUND US

PART FOUR: THE WISDOM WE'RE (STILL) LEARNING FROM THIS PANDEMIC

CONCLUSION

AFTERWORD

INTRODUCTION

"Getting old is like climbing a mountain; you may get a little out of breath, but the view is much better."
—INGRID BERGMAN

MY FRIEND MIKE IS A MILLENNIAL and I'm an old guy. The two of us have been meeting once a month for more than five years now. My role in *our* relationship is to help him be successful in life, both at home and at work. His goal is to help me help him.

Essentially, you could say I mentor him. In truth, however, we don't identify as mentor and mentee. Rather, we just call ourselves friends.

I had no idea when Mike and I began meeting that we'd become as close as we've become. I also would never have guessed that I'd be learning as much from *him* as he's learning from me. One of the many things I've learned over our years together is what makes young people tick, which is no small accomplishment, in case you don't know any Millennials. That's because that generation tends to be, well, a tad different from the rest of us, just as my generation was a bit different from the generations that preceded mine. No breaking news here.

I forgot to mention that I'm 84, which makes me 54 years older than Mike, so I have grandchildren older than him. As a result of that age gap, I've sampled a lot more of life's experiences than he has. Those experiences have added up and up, until—dare I say it?—I've become wise.

Eighty-four years in this crazy world will do that to you.

No subject is sacred when Mike and I meet. We discuss and dissect his personal life and his work life, his dreams and his visions, his mistakes and his successes. Even politics and religion are on the table. We agree to disagree and sometimes we do, but not as often as one might suspect.

Given that backdrop, here's how one of our monthly meetings went a couple of months ago...

"What's keeping you up at night?" I asked Mike, kicking off our meeting with a question. Man, do I love those questions, if you don't love questions you shouldn't try to help people. Especially young people. They like to answer questions better than they like to listen to lectures.

"Hmmm," Mike replied, leaning back in his chair. "I guess it would be...my relationship with Lisa at the office. She doesn't work directly for me, but I depend on her for marketing support."

"What's Lisa do that bugs you?"

"It isn't what she does that I'm having a problem with. It's what she doesn't do."

"Give me an example of a time when she let you down," I asked. He did.

"Mike," I said, after several more Lisa-related questions. "Have you ever heard of the 'Peter Principle?'"

Mike shook his head.

"Google it," I said. Similar to most folks his age, Mike's phone is as much an appendage as his arm. He pulled up the definition within seconds of my request: "The Peter Principle says that people in an organization tend to rise to their level of incompetence."

Then we discussed the meaning behind that definition.

"So, Mike," I asked, "is it possible that Lisa has reached her Peter Principle?" And then off we went into a wide-ranging discussion about whether or not the Peter Principle applied to Lisa and how Mike could adapt to it.

Now, if you were to ask Mike if I was "wise," I suspect he'd say yes. And yet, in the above example, all I did was ask questions. Not once did I say, "Hey Mike, here's the solution," or, "Hey Mike, here's what you need to do differently." Instead, I just kept firing questions at the poor guy until the answers popped out of his mouth.

Key distinction here. The answers popped out of *his* mouth. Not mine.

Okay, so I was familiar with the Peter Principle and how it applied to Mike's situation. But I had to let him understand it for himself. Which is, when you get right down to it, the not-so-secret formula for the sharing of wisdom. Two people, working together, asking questions, solving problems.

Being wise, I should add, is not synonymous with being smart. Mike is plenty smart. That's not the issue here. The issue is wisdom. As in experience. As in having been around the block. In my case, having been around a lot of blocks.

Speaking of smart, Mark Zuckerberg, the founder and CEO of Facebook, once made the baffling statement that, "Young people are just smarter."

"Ouch, Mark," I'd reply if I'd been there when he said it. "Wouldn't that depend on how you define the word 'smart'?' I agree that you younger folks are *smarter* about technology, but"— and then I'd pause for effect—"we old timers are *smarter* about life." Why wouldn't we be, we've been living it a lot longer than they have.

"Mark," I'd continue, still reeling from his statement, "I'm not sure you understand the difference between 'smart' and 'wise.' 'Smart' comes from genetics and books while 'wise' comes from stories and experiences." If this statement wouldn't make sense to Mark, then Facebook needs to find a new CEO.

Mike could never have asked himself the string of questions I asked because he'd never experienced the Peter Principle at work. I have and, as a matter of fact, I was even in Lisa's shoes once. (See Part One, "When All Else Fails, Face Up to the Problem—Especially When the Problem Is You.")

The path to becoming wise is littered with stories and experiences that come from the wide range of places we've been and things we've done. From school to parenting to working our jobs to reading our books to the endless internet, we end up learning something from everything we do. That list of lessons keeps adding up and up. And then finally, whether or not we set out to become wise, we arrive there.

For this book, I've chosen four pathways to becoming wise. Each pathway is filled with stories and experiences that contribute to making us old timers wise:

Part One: The Wisdom We Learn from Life

Part Two: The Wisdom We Learn from People

Part Three: The Wisdom We Learn from the World Around Us

Part Four: The Wisdom We're (Still) Learning from the Coronavirus Pandemic

I don't mean to belabor the subject, but I still can't get past Mark Zuckerberg's statement. If I had the opportunity, I'd add one more comment before I shut up. "Mark," I'd say, in my best grandfatherly voice. "Your vision is too narrow and your lens too pinched. There's a lot more to this world than the digital stuff you and your friends do."

"For people like you, being smart is only about technology," I'd conclude.

"For people like me, being wise is all about life."

THE WISDOM:

While some people may be too smart for their own good,

no one has ever been too wise for their own good.

PART ONE

The Wisdom We Learn from Life

"The two most important days in your life are the day you were born and the day you find out why."
—MARK TWAIN

IT ALL STARTS WITH MOM

*"It's not easy being a mom. If it were easy,
fathers would do it."*—BETTY WHITE

RECENTLY, I WAS TALKING WITH JULIE, a good friend from my Bend, Oregon, days, about the opening chapter of *Where Wisdom Comes From*, my initial book in this Wisdom series. In that chapter, I tell the story of my eight-year-old self. coming home from school one day and asking Mom the meaning of the word "fart." I'd heard that word at school, which is where we learned most of our swear words, along with lots of other mom-unfriendly stuff, back in those pre-internet days.

Mom then defined the word for me, followed by my asking her why she'd know the meaning of it. After all, she was a mom and I assumed moms would never do what that word meant.

"I know what that word means because it's my job to know such things," she shrugged matter-of-factly. "That's my role in life, honey. I'm here to answer your questions." Then she tousled my hair and went back to devouring her *Reader's Digest*.

In the course of Julie's feedback on the book, she said, "You know, Jim, the same thing happened to me when I was in fourth or fifth grade. My best friend at school called her teacher a bitch, and this was back in the days when that word was shockingly naughty. When I came home, I asked my mom what the word meant."

"My mom gasped when I said the word 'bitch,'" Julie continued, "and then, without further ado, grabbed my hand and pulled me into the bathroom where she washed my mouth out with soap."

"You don't know how lucky you were," Julie concluded, "to have a mom whose first impulse was to teach, no matter what the question was. My mom's first impulse was to punish."

Julie's comment was eye opening for two reasons. Firstly, I didn't think that people in the 20th century actually washed out their kid's mouths with soap. I thought that was something that moms did back in Abe Lincoln's days. My naiveté knows no bounds.

More importantly, however, her comment was eye opening because she was right. I *was* a lucky kid. My mom's first priority was to teach, the punishment would come later, after the teaching was done.

I didn't realize until I'd finished writing that first Wisdom book how many of the good things I am today are thanks to my mom— with the exception of me being the best spitball flicker in eighth grade, that is. Mom didn't teach me that, and she wasn't much help with learning how to play golf either. She pretty much sucked at that game.

And all the bad things I am? Where did those come from?

Well, some of it was the kids I ran around with, of course. The rest came from my dad.

THE WISDOM:

Friends are our accomplices, dads are our guides,

and moms are our teachers.

GROWING UP IN THE
GOOD OLD DAYS

"Those were the days when our moms put a dime in our shoe so if we got lost, we could call home. Things were different when we were growing up."—ANONYMOUS

THE FIRST VOLKSWAGEN BEETLE WAS SOLD somewhere in the U.S. back in the spring of 1949. That iconic made-in-Germany compact car cost $1,280 at the time. Kick in gas at 17¢ a gallon and you could drive anywhere and do it on the cheap. Not that my family was into traveling during those post-war times. Dad had just started a new job, one that he would remain doing until the day he retired 35 years later.

Besides the introduction of foreign cars to the American consumer, something else even bigger happened that year: Americans purchased ten million freshly invented, bulky electronic devices designed to be placed in the living room in front of the couch and plugged into a wall socket. Those devices were programmed to sell beer and Cheetos while sucking up major quantities of their owner's time.

Yes, television went mainstream in 1949.Life as we knew it would never be the same again.

The advent of TV *was* a big deal. In fact, it was the second biggest deal in America that decade. A few years earlier, our neighborhood collectively celebrated VE Day (Victory in Europe) with a bike parade, marking the end of World War II, in Europe anyway. Maybe getting our first TV didn't quite measure up to VE Day, but to this blissfully unaware 8th grader, it was close.

The impact on my family was no different than it was on any of the millions of others that would suddenly have TV thrust upon it. Deciding which program to watch became a major source of dissension.

—

"Hi Mom," I said, bursting into the kitchen after school. I'd had a hard time sitting through classes that day. "Is Dad home yet?"

"Of course he isn't, honey," she replied. "You know he doesn't get home until 5:30."

She was right, I did know that Dad wouldn't be home until 5:30, but I was setting her up. You'd think I'd have figured out that manipulating my mom was a flawed strategy. But eighth graders aren't known for their logic.

"What program do you want to watch, tonight?" I asked. Dad was bringing home our first-ever television set that night.

"Hmmm, I think maybe the Milton Berle Show," Mom said thoughtfully. "One of my bridge club friends says it's a fun program to watch." Then she turned to me with that suspicious look that moms get when they think their kid is up to something. "Why do you ask?"

"I want to watch professional wrestling," I said. "Gorgeous George is wrestling tonight."

"Gorgeous who?"

"George. C'mon, Mom, everyone knows who he is."

"I'm not everyone," she replied briskly, turning to place a casserole in the oven. In addition to everything else she did well, she was unparalleled at putting an end to a conversation that was going nowhere. We watched Milton Berle that night.

My generation was fortunate to grow up in the late 1940s and 1950s. Those were the days when such celebrities as Gorgeous George, Mickey Mantle, and Elvis Presley headlined the news and made it fun to watch TV, rather than depressing like it is today. For me, anyway.

As it turned out, our generation wasn't destined to come up with any lasting solutions to world peace, but brother, we had fun. Most of it was the sober, bright-eyed kind of fun where you wake up the next morning and remember what happened the night before (my freshman year in college excepted).

Life was mellower back then. Our music was soothingly mushy ("I'm in the Mood for Love") or gleefully irrelevant ("Zippety Do Dah"). Our favorite singers could put you to sleep (Nat King Cole) or set you on fire (Elvis). Our best times took place when the houselights were down low, unlike the 1960s, when the best times came when the searchlights were on high.

Drugs hadn't made their appearance yet, or at least they hadn't in Des Moines, Iowa, where I grew up. I can't remember one of my female classmates who had to quit school and assume motherly duties, while STDs were either nonexistent or misdiagnosed. Drive-in movies were ubiquitous and were symbolic of the times: designed for getting to first base but not to home plate.

Which kind of sums up the 1950s, when you think about it.

Here's the thing about my generation: Even today no one really knows who we are. Check it out. Even *Wikipedia* isn't sure how people my age earned our Silent Generation designation or what it's supposed to mean. The only thing that *Wikipedia* does know is that we're sandwiched between the Greatest Generation (our predecessors) and the Baby Boomers (our successors). Maybe we should have been dubbed the Overlooked Generation.

I can still remember Mom shaking her head and telling me and my sister, Chris, about the travails of the Great Depression and the pain and dysfunction that came from World War II. She and Dad had so much more heartache and drama in their lives than Chris and I had in ours. On second thought, maybe we should have been called the Lucky Generation. *Wikipedia*, take note.

One of the reasons my generation spent so much time doing the innocent kind of stuff we did was that we didn't have to worry about social injustice. We'd learn in later years that there was plenty of it to worry about: racial discrimination, gender inequalities, and so much more. But TV was just getting started and Twitter and Facebook hadn't been invented yet, so the world wasn't awash in information like it is today. Which can be a good thing.

Perhaps it was those carefree growing-up days that defined our mellow behavior, although it may have been the other way around. Maybe us kids in the 1940s and 1950s were simply wired differently than those who came along in the 1960s. There was plenty of trouble we could have stirred up if we had looked hard enough. We were probably too busy to stir it up. Or maybe too tired.

Instead of having to fight a war or screw caps on milk bottles (which is what my dad did during the Great Depression), we'd graduate from high school or college and go on to careers that included, in most cases, jobs that were as good or better than our parents had. We were also free to spend our time focused on working or playing or raising our kids. There were no wars to fight or breadlines to stand in.

There is one noteworthy thing we did accomplish back in those years: We raised the kids who went on to become the Baby Boomers. Their generation would set the stage for where our country, and those of us who trailed behind them, find ourselves today: a long way from perfect but a better place than our parents had.

THE WISDOM:

Better that our childhood be filled with hopscotch,

jacks, and jump-rope, than the number of

Facebook likes or the smartness of cellphones.

THE WAY KIDS' SPORTS OUGHTA BE

"If you want your children to keep their feet on the ground, put some responsibility on their shoulders."
—ABAGAIL VAN BUREN

LET IT BE KNOWN THAT I'M one of those guys who coached his kid's sport teams, year in and year out—mostly football and hockey, but I also did stints in basketball and baseball. I wasn't one of those yeller, screamer, referee baiter types. I did my best to remind my kids that sports aren't about winning or losing. They're about building character.

Okay, so I did my best to help my teams win. It's more fun to win than to lose, in sports and in life.

Over my coaching years, I saw the good, the bad, and the ugly. The good ranged from the smiles and hugs of teammates following a hard-fought game to the thanks of parents for positively impacting their kid's life. Those two gifts alone are what make coaching worthwhile.

But I also witnessed the bad and the ugly, from a coach squirting mosquito repellent in the face of an umpire to another coach screaming at one of his team members until the tears rained down the kid's face. What is it about adults? Why can't we vent our frustrations somewhere else? Our kids have enough trouble growing up without us making things worse.

Notwithstanding the downsides of kid's sports, the upsides make them worth the time and effort—especially when the role of adults can be minimized while maximizing the role of the kids.

———

It was late in the summer of 1947; I'd be entering sixth grade that year. A bunch of us kids decided to start our own football team. So we did, and, as it turned out, while we didn't learn a lot about the game of football from that experience, we sure learned how to turn an idea into a reality. Without the help of adults.

It was my friend Randy who kicked it off by convincing us that Hubbell Elementary School needed a football team. Since ninth grade was the first year of organized football in Des Moines, the idea of sixth graders playing the game was a novel one. Nevertheless, Randy—probably because he was early adopter in becoming an alpha male—picked up the phone and let his fingers do the dialing. Within a few days, the Hubbell Hawks were born.

There were eleven of us on that team. In order to be guaranteed a position, we had to promise we wouldn't get sick on Saturdays, since you can't field a football team with ten kids. That meant we had to show up even when we weren't feeling so hot. It was a lesson some of us would carry on into our adult years.

We needed a coach, so we talked a kid who was on the high school football team into teaching us how to block, tackle, and draw up plays. Sometimes the coach would show up for practice and sometimes he wouldn't, but he was there often enough to help us get the Hawks off the ground. Besides, we had more fun with him than we would have had with a real live adult.

Once we had a team, we needed someone to play. Randy went back to the phone again. "Hey Ron," he'd pitch. "Are you Perkins guys too chicken shit to play us Hubbell guys in football?" Which was all that it took; within a few days we had a two-team league. By the time October rolled around, we'd rounded up two more teams. Our makeshift league now included the Hawks, Perkins

Elementary, St. Augustine (a nearby Catholic school), and a team from the local Jewish synagogue. Talk about diversity.

Our uniforms were whatever our moms allowed us to wear that was deemed okay to rip, tear, and ruin. My gear included a World War II aviator hat, complete with ear holes and wool-lined chin strap. I was one of the few who had shoulder pads; as the shrimpiest kid on the team, I needed them. Three of the Hawk players had leather helmets and one even had one of those newfangled plastic ones. There was also a stocking cap or two on the team; meanwhile Dave Readinger went bare headed. The Amateur Athletic Union would have disqualified us had they known.

I was the smallest and skinniest kid on the team so I was assigned the right guard position, the equivalent of being the right fielder in baseball. Both are positions where you stick the more untalented kids and hope they'll do the least harm. I was assured inclusion on the team when my mom volunteered to furnish chocolate chip cookies for our Saturday morning games.

Quarterback is the sexiest position on a football team and Bill, a kid who lived down the street, was awarded that position. He didn't have the best throwing arm and he wasn't the best leader, but he did have one major qualification: he owned the best football. Such was our early lesson on the backhanded ways that capitalism works.

We played and practiced on a vacant piece of land that belonged to our high school and included a baseball diamond at the far end. The field was maybe a hundred yards long, although maybe it wasn't. A couple of dowel rods and a ten-foot rope served as the first-down marker; four orange cones marked the respective goal lines. And that would be it for the capital expenditures required to field one sixth-grade football team in 1947. We played without referees, shouting, shoving, and reluctant compromising somehow resolved all disputes.

Fans in the stands? There weren't any stands so there weren't many fans. Parents like fancy uniforms and a place to sit down and the Hawks offered neither. As it turned out, our parents weren't missed. We saw enough of them at home.

We played Perkins twice that year and the other two teams once. We won all four games, although the outcome of the second game with a fired-up Perkins team is in dispute—or so I recently learned when I called Joe, a former Hawks team member with a better memory than mine. The details of that game are sketchy. In the absence of proof to the contrary, I'll state for the record that we won that one too.

In the end, our spur-of-the-moment team turned out to be a rip-roaring success. Best of all, we had fun. So we did it again in seventh grade.

That same year I also played on an official Little League baseball team, replete with fancy uniforms, hollering coaches, and noisy parents. From that experience I learned how to be part of a team.

From my Hawks' experience, I learned how to build one.

THE WISDOM:

It's better for kids to make their own tracks than

follow someone else's.

TWO WORDS YOU GOTTA LOVE: FREE BEER!

"You can't be a real country unless you have a beer and an airline—it helps if you have some kind of football team, or some nuclear weapons, but in the very least you need beer."—FRANK ZAPPA

IT WAS 1955 AND I WAS a freshman at the University of Colorado. An immature, flighty freshman, I should add, as you're about to learn from the following story...

—

FREE BEER!

I'm not kidding, that's what the sign said on the wall outside my ROTC class; the exact words were "Free Beer for all ROTC students." The sign might just as well have said "Free Beer for All Immature College Freshmen." Either way, you could count me in.

You could count my buddy Brains in, too. We went to the same high school in Des Moines, and Brains was my best friend at the University of Colorado that year; he was in the Navy ROTC program while I was in the Air Force one. His nickname was Brains partly because he had a huge one and also because his last name was Brainerd. On most occasions, his huge brain opted to do the right thing, which meant that he was my mom's favorite among all my friends.

But owners of huge brains are capable of doing stupid things too, just not as often as us medium-brained folks. So off Brains and I went to the upstairs room of the Tulagi Bar in Boulder on the eve of the much-awaited free-beer offer. We had from 5pm to 7pm to drink as much Coors as we could swallow.

Fun Fact: In those days, you could drink beer legally in Boulder at age 18, which is the one of the primary reasons I chose to go to college there. I can't remember what the other reasons were.

Second Fun Fact: Thanks to logic I'm incapable of explaining, free beer always tastes better than beer you pay for. It goes down faster, too.

By seven o'clock we'd drained our last pitcher. Brains and I staggered out of Tulagi's and into his car. Remember, this was 1955, and while drunk driving was a thing back then, it wasn't maniacally enforced.

"Les' go to Denver," I slurred.

"Wha'for?" replied Brains.

"I wanna see Larimer Street." Larimer Street was, back in those days, the center of Denver's dive bar scene. Brains and I would be among friends.

So off we went. Brains was driving, that much I can remember. The rest of the experience is foggy.

For instance, I don't remember arriving at Larimer Street. And I don't remember Brains telling me he was tired and going home, with or without me. I also don't remember disturbing anyone's peace, but I do remember being tossed in the back of a Denver police van with a bunch of other drunken idiots.

I also remember, like it was yesterday, slinking against the wall in the "drunk tank" of Denver's jail, in company with a dozen or so of the orneriest drunks in Colorado, several of whom didn't take kindly to snot-nosed college kids. And I do remember, clear as a bell, the fight that broke out between a couple of those ornery drunks, with a crowd of Denver's finest, laughing and egging them on.

The following morning I was sent on my way, frightened but wiser. My wallet, I quickly discovered, was emptier than a freshman college students' head and it was pouring rain as I slunk out of the jail building and back to the freedom of Denver's downtown streets. Four hours later, following a lot of sodden walking and a couple of hitchhiking rides, I was back in Boulder. Tired, wet, and worried stiff.

I was worried stiff because, as a result of my jail experience, I faced two looming problems. First, if the ROTC mucky mucks were to find out what had happened last night, I could be booted from the program. Second, if my mom found out, I could be dead.

My savior was Master Sergeant Kelly who handled all the admin stuff for our ROTC unit and also knew his away around life. He'd been young once too, he scolded. He then got busy and helped me cover my guilty ass. "You won't be able to run for President anytime soon," he advised, "but you can still fly our country's airplanes."

I won't say that was the last time I overdid the consumption of alcohol in my life, but I will say it was the last time I visited Larimer Street, or places like it, when I was logic impaired. Some lessons we learn the hard way.

Years later, when the time was exactly right, I told Mom about my Larimer Street experience.

"Sometimes I wonder," she said, cupping my head in her tiny hands, "why it took you so long to grow up."

Me too, Mom. Me too.

THE WISDOM:

No good ever comes from too much alcohol…well,

that I can remember, anyway.

NOTE TO WOMEN:
DON'T DEPEND ON MEN TO
SOLVE YOUR PROBLEMS

"I'm done. I'm done competing with other women."
—SALLIE KRAWCHECK

FRESHLY MARRIED, I GRADUATED FROM THE University of Colorado in 1958. Thanks to being paid by the government to attend four years of ROTC classes, it was now payback time; I owed the Air Force three years of my life. Surprisingly, those three years turned out to be a positive experience and I still feel a tinge of pride for having served in the military, even though no one ever shot at me.

You don't have to be a hero to feel good about serving your country.

Upon reporting for duty, the first thing I did was flunk the hearing test required to fly the Air Force's hallowed airplanes. Since flying had been the sole reason I signed up for ROTC in the first place, this was not a positive outcome. But I was still an Air Force guy, so the powers that be decided I'd make a good Accounting and Finance officer. Following nine months of training, I was deployed to a small air base in Klamath Falls, Oregon. My assignment? Pay 2,000 people twice a month, maintain their pay records, and manage an office of twenty-four enlisted men and six civilian women.

Remember, I was twenty-two years old at the time and knew nothing about managing people. Which meant, of course, that I thought it would be a snap. For those unfamiliar with the military, you must first understand that freshly christened 2nd Lieutenants have a reputation for wide-eyed innocence. I was their poster child.

As it turned out, the financial part of my job was easy. The people management part? Not so much. The twenty-four enlisted men were a cinch to supervise: The culture in the military requires that they do what they're told, whether or not their boss is a mature and rational adult.

My management problems were with the six civilians in the office, all of whom were women. More specifically, the problem was with Dorothy, the dark-haired, fiery, outspoken one, and Shirley, the quiet, thoughtful, introspective one. Both were smart, efficient, and contributing team members.

Well, they were contributing team members when working with the rest of the folks in the office, anyway, but they could barely speak to one another without spitting.

While I'd been duly trained in accounting and finance matters, I hadn't been trained to solve complex communication problems, especially between two women. No matter. I dove in anyway, figuring logic and common sense would prevail. Dorothy, Shirley and I would sit down, discuss the symptoms, identify the problems, and come up with a solution. End of story. Time to move on.

Dream on, Jim.

"Ladies," I said, starting the meeting. "Both of you are important to our office. You both care about your work, you both are professional, and you both get along with the rest of the team. But you don't get along with each other. We need to address this issue. What are your thoughts on how we should proceed?"

Silence.

"Hmmm. OK, let's talk about what's happening here," I said, deciding to take a new tack. "What do either of you think the underlying problem is between the two of you?"

Silence.

Oh, oh. Switching tactics, I decided I'd make it so they *had* to reply to my question. "OK, Dorothy, what do *you* think the problem is?"

"She's a bitch," Dorothy said.

"She's an asshole," Shirley hissed without being asked.

Whoa. My training didn't include this.

"Dorothy and Shirley," I said, shakily. "This situation makes no sense to me. You're both pleasant people, you both do good work, and you both work well with the rest of the office. I don't understand why you can't be friends, or at least amiable co-workers."

"She'd still be a bitch."Dorothy said.

"She'd still be an asshole," Shirley replied, on cue.

My memory fails me as to who said what next. Somehow the meeting ended, and aside from my ego, there were no visible injuries. Nor was there a resolution. Shirley and Dorothy would unhappily co-exist for the remaining two years I was stationed in Klamath Falls.

Fast forward to the early 2000s.

I was working with my friend Linda on a business assistance program in Bend. She was an ex-Microsofter who had been there during its early wild-wild-west days. We were discussing workplace conflict, so I told her my Shirley and Dorothy story.

"That's the way it was at Microsoft, too, when I was there. We women got along fine with the guys, but we fought like hell with each other."

"But that was then, and this is now," she continued. "Thankfully, we're starting to figure out that we need to play in the same sandbox with our female peers. That we're better when we're working together than we are when we're tearing each other apart."

"No offense, Jim," she concluded with a thin smile, "but we've finally learned we can solve our problems ourselves. Without the help of a man."

THE WISDOM:

Wars were invented because men couldn't solve

their own problems. Why would women depend

on them to solve theirs?

PLAYING THE MARKET WITH THE PROS

"One of the funny things about the stock market is that every time one person buys, another sells, and both think they are astute."—WILLIAM FEATHER

GRANDPA JOE, MOM'S DAD, LIVED A hard life. He grew up in the tiny town of Blakesburg, Iowa (population today: 289), where he worked a small farm while raising a large family. Feeding and educating six kids—three boys and three girls—in the early 1900s was not for the faint of heart, especially for an uneducated farmer, the son of a Tyrolean immigrant.

Somehow, he raised each of his children to be contributing adults—but not without paying a price. His wife Alma died soon after the arrival of their sixth child and, like many people who grow old alone, Joe became cranky and irksome. His kids were not immune to his moods. While our family would frequently visit my Dad's mom who lived in her own small town of Perry, Iowa, we rarely made the two-hour drive to Blakesburg to see Grandpa Joe. He probably preferred it that way.

One by one, Joe's kids waved goodbye to Blakesburg following high school. Only one of the six, his youngest daughter, hung around to take over the family farm. Joe's oldest son, Bill, won an appointment to the U.S. Naval Academy and went on to become a highly decorated navy pilot and ultimately a three-star admiral.

My mom, meanwhile, graduated from Iowa State College and did a short stint as a high school math teacher before doing what most women did back in those days: have kids and stay home.

I was fresh out of the Air Force and working a job I hated in Moline, Illinois, when Grandpa Joe passed away in 1963. Blakesburg was only a two-hour drive from Moline, and so on a hot, muggy Saturday afternoon in late June, I made the drive to attend Joe's funeral. It was the only time I'd seen all of Mom's five siblings in the same room. To my knowledge, it was also the last time the family would all be together at the same time.

Following the service, we headed for the weathered farm where the kids had grown up and where their youngest sister now lived. I can still remember the tiny, tired, sparsely furnished house with the linoleum floor in the kitchen that creaked, squeaked, and buckled when someone walked by.

I glommed on to Uncle Bill as soon as we walked into the house. The two of us sat in the kitchen, snacking on potato salad and listening to the floor squeak while I barraged him with questions about his life in the Navy. At an earlier point in his career, he'd been the skipper of the USS Ticonderoga, an aircraft carrier that had seen action in World War II. One of the highlights of my dad's life had been when, at Uncle Bill's invitation, he got to spend three days on the Ticonderoga while it was on maneuvers. "When I was at sea on the Ticonderoga..." Dad would begin, and then off he'd go, reliving those memorable days.

At the time of the funeral, Uncle Bill was stationed in Washington, D.C., and was the Director of Material for the Navy, which meant he was in charge of buying stuff. Big, expensive stuff, like battleships and destroyers and aircraft carriers. And airplanes too, which led him, after a few leading questions from me, to confide that the Navy would be announcing, on the following Tuesday, the purchase of several billion dollars of fighter aircraft from Department of Defense contractor Ling- Temco-Vought. That's billions, with a B.

Was this a news scoop I just heard? Did this make me a Wall Street insider? After all, I knew something the rest of the financial world didn't, or so I surmised anyway. Not only that, what I knew came straight from the horse's mouth. This was mouthwatering information for a kid who was making chump change working for a bank.

I raced home after saying goodbye to the Schoech (pronounced "Shay") siblings, and, once back in Moline, called my friend Hap. Hap was a stockbroker, otherwise known these days as a financial advisor. I told him about my inside scoop.

"We gotta buy Ling-Temco-Vaught stock the first thing on Monday morning," I said. "I think I can borrow the money from my mother-in-law."

The next morning, I borrowed $2,500 from my wife's mom and Hap made the purchase late Monday afternoon. We bought LTV (the ticker symbol for Ling-Temco-Vaught) at $18 a share. Tuesday morning came, I feigned a doctor's appointment and headed straight for Hap's office. Pulling up a chair where I could watch the ticker tape roll by, I waited for LTV to come streaming across.

And sure enough it came, just as I'd dreamed it would. The news had been officially announced that morning and for the first few hours the tape was filled with LTV trades. My first stock experience as an insider! I can still remember telling myself that I could get used to this kind of work. It sure beat the hell out of making seven bucks an hour working for a bank. LTV opened the day at $19 a share and closed at $22.

While Tuesday was a spectacular day for LTV's investors, Wednesday came and the tide turned. The awesomeness of Tuesday turned into the awfulness of Wednesday as my LTV stock snaked down and down, trade by trade, ending the day back at $18, right where I'd bought it. Which is where it would languish until a week or so later when I sold it at $17.

I later learned that, while the Navy had announced the LTV transaction on Tuesday just as Uncle Bill had said it would, the traders had heard the rumor long before the formal announcement was made. (Who can keep a secret in Washington, D.C.?). As a result, the pros purchased LTV at somewhere around $14 early on and then sold it on Tuesday afternoon when it topped out at $22.

Which is why people like them are called pros.

And why people like me are called amateurs.

THE WISDOM:

It's not what you know when you bet money on the

stock market, it's when you know it.

HOW TO FIND A CAREER YOU CAN LOVE

"My son is now an entrepreneur. That's what it's called when you don't have a job."—TED TURNER

BEFORE WE GET STARTED, HERE ARE three career-related questions for you to ponder:

1. How old were you when you first began thinking about your dream career?
2. How old were you when you started the job you hoped would end up being your dream career?
3. How old were you when you finally found the job that actually turned into your dream career? (Or are you one of the unlucky ones who never found it?)

If you're like most folks, you probably started thinking about your dream career in your final years of high school. Some may have known exactly what they wanted to do and went on to careers in law, medicine, social service, government, farming, or the military. Others, like me, knew they needed to be in the "business" sector, but had no idea what kind of business would be best for them. Fortune 500? Public? Private? Small business? Home business?

Also, back in those days, we job seekers envisioned pursuing a business career for thirty years, then doing what most people set out to do when they started working in the first place: Retire. With a pension, of course.

Such was the linear sequence I expected, as did my father's generation. But it wouldn't turn out to be that way for me. It took me sixteen years following high school graduation to find the career I'd eventually love. Ultimately, those sixteen years paid off, and I would go on to love *almost* every minute of my entrepreneur career.

My path to that career was not linear, however. Ultimately, it would be a resounding failure that led me to where I belonged.

—

Following college, I bounced from job to job. First it was the Air Force, then banking, and finally I landed at St. Regis Paper, becoming one of the 60,000 employees at that high and mighty Fortune 500 company.

It was at St. Regis where my troubles began. After two years as their dependable and trusty forty-hour-a-week employee, I had a vision about how the division I worked for could build ice arenas. Affordable ice arenas. The roofs would be of geodesic dome design with the struts consisting of wooden fence posts that were—surprise, surprise—one of the products my division manufactured.

Brilliant idea, right? A roof held up by inexpensive fence posts. Geodesic dome design. First of its kind in the world.

Well, it would also turn out to be the last of its kind in the world. Assembling the damn thing was a nightmare. An expensive nightmare.

That ice arena was eventually built however, and I was never told how much money the project cost. St. Regis didn't fire me, although I have no idea why; I'd have fired me if I were them. Soon thereafter I left of my own accord.

From that experience I learned that I loved pursuing a vision. I also learned that I loved change and enjoyed taking risks. Most of all, I learned that I no longer wanted to have someone else telling me what to do. I needed to be telling myself.

I needed to be my own boss.

Back in those days, people who started or owned their own small businesses were called exactly that: small business owners. Or sometimes mom-and-pops. The word "entrepreneur" didn't become part of America's lexicon until the early 1970s.

Steve Jobs, one of the world's all-time most successful entrepreneurs, once said when speaking to an audience of people like himself, "Here's to us, to the crazy ones. The misfits, the rebels, the ones who see the world differently."

Jobs didn't say, "Here's to the crazy ones who couldn't hold down a job," but he may just as well have. I was one of the crazy ones. What employer in his or her right mind would want to hire someone like me?

The truth is, people like me make lousy employees. Don't hire us.

To further prove Job's crazy-one's point, shortly following the ice arena experience, I bought a sporting goods business that had previously been in bankruptcy, which meant it had already been screwed up by someone else. Enter me to screw it up even more. At the beginning, anyway.

In order to buy that business in the first place, I needed to borrow money from my mom (recently widowed) and five friends. Note: If you're ever looking to stoke your motivation to succeed, try owing money to your friends or, God forbid, to your mom. You'll run through walls to pay them back.

I had a stay-at-home wife and three hungry sons with nary a pot to pee in at the time I bought that business, and yet I bought it anyway. I couldn't help what I did, I'd caught the small business bug and would go on to start three more Minneapolis-based businesses over the next seven years.

In addition to being one of the crazy ones, I also turned out to be one of the lucky ones. Finally, at the ripe old age of 33, I stumbled on the career that was made for me. The career I could love.

Never mind that it took losing a boatload of St. Regis's money to find it.

THE WISDOM:

One thing the millennials have right;

don't work at a job you can't love. Keep looking

until you find one you can.

WHEN ALL ELSE FAILS, FACE UP TO THE PROBLEM—ESPECIALLY WHEN THE PROBLEM IS YOU

"The question 'Who Ought to Be Boss?' is like asking 'Who ought to be the tenor in a quartet?' Obviously, the man who can sing tenor."—HENRY FORD

I'D BE WILLING TO BET THAT just about every American has, at one time or another, thought about taking the leap and starting his or her own business. The Small Business Administration tells us there are thirty million small businesses in the U.S. in a nation of almost 330 million. If that number is correct, this means a whopping one out of every eleven Americans owns a small business.

As discussed in the preceding chapter, most of us who have taken the leap did so primarily because we needed to be our own boss. We thought our work would be more successful—and fun—if we were the ones calling the shots.

In my case, anyway, I wasn't disappointed. Work *was* more fun, especially in the early days when the business was small, scrappy, and could turn on a dime.

For instance, here's how I'd spend a typical morning back in the formative days of owning a business:

8AM   Meet with the president of ABC Corporation to iron out the details of winning their business.

9AM   Meet with a freelance graphic designer to discuss a spiffy new ad campaign she was designing for us.

10AM   Meet with my sales guy to discuss a new product to offer our customers.

11AM   Make a sales call to the CEO of MNOP Corporation, who'd heard about my company from the CEO of XYZ Corporation.

This was how scrappy small businesses worked for their owners in their formative years. We got to spend our time working on the creative and exciting stuff that made our business pop and that got our adrenalin running.

Now, fast forward fifteen years from the time my business was small and scrappy. Against all odds, the business was flourishing, and I had a team of professional and ably performing employees working for, and with, me.

Here's a snapshot of a typical day at the office now:

8AM   Meet with Bill from Accounting, who heard through the office grapevine that Helen from Marketing is making a dollar more an hour than he is. He believes he is a victim of reverse discrimination and wants to know what I am going to do about it.

9AM   Meet with Frank, our insurance consultant, who wants to discuss the settlement we should offer to the driver of the car our delivery truck rear-ended.

10AM   Meet with Angie, our Director of Human Resources, who wants to discuss a sexual harassment lawsuit filed against one of our employees.

11AM   Meet with a representative from our financial services provider, who wants to discuss the latest tax law changes and how they'll impact our 401 (k) plans.

In short, over that span of fifteen years, I morphed from being an entrepreneur into being a manager—an unhappy and malcontented manager, to be more precise. I was now spending the majority of my waking hours solving problems, most of which were related to people: Good old irascible, weird, unpredictable, never-a-dull-moment people. People who sapped my energy and tried my patience and took all the fun out of my work.

Now don't get me wrong. I'm aware that a business—or any organization, for that matter—wins or loses because of the people who are employed by it. And you gotta solve your employees' problems in order to create an environment for them to succeed. If you don't, the good ones will go away.

However, like 99.9% of my peers, I'd rather be out where the action is—working on new products, discovering new markets, meeting with new customers—as opposed to dealing with the problems that come out of the minds of employees.

Or, stated another way, I want to be working on where the business is going rather than on where it's been.

Here, then, is what happened after my entrepreneur-turned-manger role turned sour. One hot summer day in Minneapolis, following yet another morning of mind-draining meetings, I decided I'd had enough. So I slouched out of my office, slid into my car, and drove to the nearest park. Finding an inviting bench alongside a picnic table, I pulled out paper and pen, and made a list of all the reasons why I was a lousy manager.

The list included:

Attention to detail. I hate details.
Focus. I'd rather bounce from project to project than focus on one.
Patience. I'm way too busy to be patient.
Conflict. I don't like conflict, so I don't address it.
Consistency. I never do things the same way twice.

As a result of making this list of my managerial deficiencies that afternoon, I decided I needed to make a major change in my life. After fifteen years of running that business, I'd hire a manager to run it. A manager who enjoyed doing all that people-management stuff that was making my life miserable.

And that's not all I'd do. In order to make room for that manager, I'd make one more key change.

I'd fire the guy whose place he took.

So, I did it. I fired myself.

THE WISDOM:

Never beat a dead horse, especially when that

dead horse is you.

WHAT TO DO WHEN RETIREMENT DOESN'T WORK

"For the unlearned, old age is winter; for the learned, it is the season of the harvest." ~HASIDIC SAYING

IN 1990, A FEW MONTHS BEFORE my 54th birthday, I sold my fourth and final Minneapolis business, effectively concluding the first half of my life. The first half was the "Learn and Earn" part and consisted of raising kids, starting a business, and trying to save enough money to fund retirement.

The second half, according to American custom, would be the "Retirement" years, or whatever you choose to call the time when the Learn and Earn years are finished. So, kicking off that second half of our lives, Mary and I hightailed it off to San Diego where the sun was bright, the weather warm, and the ocean only a stone's throw away.

In essence, I retired—or so I intended to do at the time. Meanwhile, Mary was working remotely for a Minneapolis-based company.

The first couple of weeks of retirement almost killed me. Or, rather, it almost got me killed. It didn't take Mary long to get tired of me clomping around the house looking for something to do. Killing me surely must have crossed her mind.

To make matters worse, my golf game turned south, which is not what's supposed to happen when you work hard at something for six hours a day, seven days a week. My waistline also expanded, my energy level shrunk, and opening the mail became the highlight of my day.

Sundays were the worst. There wasn't any mail.

"Go find something to do," Mary said. "Fix something. Start a business. Get a job."

Since I'm a hopeless non-fixer, especially around the house, that suggestion was dead in the water. I'd also started four businesses over the last 20 years, so I'd had enough of that. Getting a job seemed to be my only option, except that the thought of having a boss ultimately put the kibosh on that one too. Finally, I decided there'd be a fourth option, one of my own making.

"I know, I'll be a writer," I announced to Mary one morning. "I'll write books, articles, even newsletters. Who knows, I might even get paid."

I knew I could write; I'd had plenty of practice. I was known as "Mr. Memo" back in my pre-internet, pre-email, business days. I could crank out company-wide epistles at the drop of a hat on subjects ranging from the direction of our business to our latest products to the state of the universe. If I could write for my employees, why couldn't I write for regular people too?

Thanks to the introduction of desktop computers and their word processing functions, I figured writing would be easy. Computers weren't exactly ubiquitous back in those days, but I had an early model (a Zenith) and I knew how to make its keyboard hum. The trick was getting whatever it was you wrote published so that people could read it, which was a lot bigger trick then than it is these days. Now, thanks to Amazon and the proliferation of self-publishing, anyone can get published.

Even with that new career however, I still had a problem filling my day. If I'm out of bed at 6am and write hard for four hours, I'm brain dead by 10am. A 30-minute nap and with dinner scheduled for 6ish, I'd still have 7½ hours to kill.I decided to supplement writing with two more careers: volunteering and mentoring, in addition to pursuing the golf hobby that Mary and I were enjoying together.

I'm not saying that my version of retirement—or non-retirement, as it turned out to be—is for everyone. But I am saying there are all kinds of options in the second half of our lives other than golf, TV, or visiting the grandkids.

Here are some of the options available for those of you who aren't into a traditional retirement:

Play bridge or chess. Twenty-five million Americans play bridge. Fifteen million play chess. They're both effective brain-oiling pastimes. Thanks to the internet, you can play them anytime, including in the middle of the night and during pandemics.

Play pickleball. Only 3 million Americans currently play pickleball, but that number is increasing by 10% every year, which makes it the fastest-growing sport in America. It's quick and it's fun and it's social and it's inexpensive. And it's a hell of a lot easier game to play than tennis.

Join a club. Book clubs, financial clubs, astronomy clubs, hiking clubs, gardening clubs, basket-weaving club, makers spaces…there's something out there for everyone. My sister Chris, along with Woody her wonder dog, joined a Denver Flyball Club until Woody aged out. Chris was in her early 70s at the time.

Move to a foreign country. Home sweet home doesn't have to be in the U.S. Mary and I considered New Zealand way back in 1990 until we determined they didn't need ex-entrepreneurs (me) or ex-sales managers (Mary).

Go rural. Move to the country or to a small town. We chose Bend in 1994. It was home to 30,000 people at the time and almost as many dogs. Smaller is better, for some people anyway, and it sure was for us. It was also quieter. And safer. The golf, skiing, and fly-fishing weren't too shabby either.

Build a bucket list and then develop a plan to empty it.
The building part can be as fun as the emptying.
Go back to school. Check out the Bernard Osher Foundation on YouTube for cool, affordable options. Learn stuff you don't know while, at the same time, feel like you're young again.
Explore YouTube. Every day a billion or so—that's with a "B"—learning-related videos are viewed on YouTube. Try TedTalks or the Socratic Method or SmarterEveryDay. Or just type in "learning opportunities" on your favorite search bar. All kinds of cool options will pop up.

You'll note I didn't include "play golf" on this list. If you've been a golfer in the first half of your life, you'll continue to play the game in the second half. You won't need any prompting from me.

If you haven't been a golfer, don't start now. Unless, that is, you're looking for a fresh source of frustration and a new way to spend money.

THE WISDOM:

Just because your work is done shouldn't mean it's

time for your brain to retire.

IF YOU'RE NOT RETIRED, THEN WHAT ARE YOU?

"A society grows great when old men plant trees in whose shade they never will sit."—GREEK PROVERB

I HAVE JUST ENOUGH HAIR TO require a haircut every two months or so. A better word would be "hair trim" because the top of my head is a marble-top wasteland where nothing but stray weeds grow. Yet every month I shell out $18 ($13 plus tip) to keep a few rogue hairs from covering my ears. I'm not implying that I regret either the time or the money I spend at the barbershop; oftentimes it can be entertaining.

But not all the time. Especially when I run into Ed.

—

"Hi Jim, long time no see," I heard a voice say as I entered the barbershop. I looked up to see Ed, waiting to get his hair cut. Ed plays golf at the same course I do.

"How ya doin', buddy?" Ed asked. "Haven't seen you in a coon's age." My name isn't "buddy" and what *is* a coon's age, anyway? I rolled my eyes hoping Ed would take the bait.

No luck. "Whatcha been up to, pal?" he asked.

"Oh, the usual," I shrugged. I'm never quite sure how to answer that question.I eat, I sleep, I volunteer, and I mind my own business. Ed should try the last two sometime.

Just to clarify, I never say, "I'm retired" when someone asks me Ed's question. That's because I'm not. Nor do I wish to be. Ever.

So now you know.

"I worry about you, Jim. You oughta be spending more time on the golf course," Ed droned on. "You're old enough to be retired. You need to start acting like it."

"I have no intention of retiring, Ed," I huffed, "you need to get over it."

"Well, if you're not retired, then what are you?" Ed asked, a smirk on his pasty lips. He wasn't going to quit bugging me, a sure sign of someone who *is* retired.

However, Ed did ask an interesting question. If I'm not retired, then what am I?

Whatever it is I am, I'm not alone. A recent Mass Mutual study revealed that 72% of our nation's retirees report being "extremely or quite happy" doing whatever retired people do. Meanwhile, I'm part of the other 28%—those folks who are of "retirement age" but don't want to be retired. That number represents millions of Americans, all of whom must be either bored or doing something other than being retired in their post-employment years.

I suppose it's only a matter of semantics about what people like me should be called, but no one has figured it out yet. Be my guest if you'd like to try, but first you'll need to consider the meaning of the word "retired." Here's how *Dictionary.com* and *Merriam-Webster's Dictionary* define it:

Dictionary.com: Retired; withdrawn from, or no longer occupied with, one's business or profession."

Merriam-Webster's Dictionary: Retired; withdrawn from one's position or occupation: having concluded one's working or professional career.

Whoa now, *Dictionary.com* and *Merriam-Webster's Dictionary* both use the word "withdrawn" in defining the word "retired." To me, that word has a negative connotation. I mean, who wants to be known as being withdrawn?

"Hi, I'm Jim. I'm withdrawn."

So, I looked up the antonym to "withdrawn." It's "advanced." Or "engaged." Or "involved." Or "engrossed." All positive words, words that denote enthusiasm and passion and making stuff happen. Personally, I'd rather be known as "involved" than "withdrawn." Wouldn't most folks?

The majority of us who are not like Ed and who have no desire to be withdrawn want—no, we actually *need*—to be something else. Rewired, or re-inspired, or renewed, or re-energized, or re-focused, or whatever you want to call people who fail at retiring.

Marc Freedman, in his need-to-read book *The Big Shift,* talks at length about this topic but doesn't come up with a suitable name for us oldsters who are essentially unretired. I'm sure he must have considered using the word "elder" but decided against it. Good move with that, Marc.

Freedman does, however, come up with a name for what unretired people of retirement age do. He says that that the 28% of us who decide we need to stay involved and meaningfully engaged after finishing our working careers are pursuing our "encore career." He defines that term as "work in the second half of life that combines possibly income, greater personal meaning, and/or making a social impact."

When I think of Freedman's definition, up pops the image of Jimmy Carter, the poster geezer for those of us who are among the "unretired retired" and have, in many cases, accomplished more in our encore careers than we did in our working ones. That's Carter, for sure.

We may not know what to call ourselves, but we damn well know what we do.

THE WISDOM:

Retirement may be a never-ending vacation, but a vacation from what? Hopefully not from learning, relevance, or making our world a better place.

FOR THE LOVE OF A DOG

"You want a friend in Washington? Get a dog."
PRESIDENT HARRY S. TRUMAN

ONCE THE KIDS HAVE LEFT HOME, the house turns quiet. Too quiet, for many of us. We need some commotion in our lives. A wee bit of chaos here and there. Enter…the dog. Or, in our house…the dogs. At one time we had four, today we're down to two.

Which makes Mary and I experts on the subject of dogs. For instance…

———

Let's say you're driving down the street and you spot someone on the sidewalk walking towards you with a dog on a leash. As you whiz by, you take a sideways glance in their direction. You don't have time to look at both the person and the dog, so which do you choose? The person or the dog?

Which is how you can tell whether or not you're a dog lover. Even a hardcore dog lover. If you are one, you'll check out the dog first. After all—gender aside—most dog walkers look somewhat the same: a baseball cap here, a Nike T-shirt there, a poop bag dangling from their back pocket.

Not so with dogs. There are no lookalikes where dogs are concerned. An Aussie doesn't look like a Great Dane and a Labradoodle can't double for a Pit Bull. Most dog people are suckers for one breed or another, why, I know people who think Pugs are the coolest dogs in town. I know, hard to believe.

Mary and I are mutt people. All of our dogs are rescues and all have come from animal shelters. Muttness runs in our family.

This driving-down-the-street scenario can change, of course, if the driver of the car is Mary and the guy with the dog happens to be Hugh Jackman. Somehow, she'd know to look at him first. Or if the driver is me and Scarlett Johansson is on the tall end of the leash. But you get the point. Most of the time, for those of us who are really, truly dog lovers, we only have eyes for the pup.

Getting back to the Scarlett Johansson scenario, let's say your dog Boris is on your leash and the two of you spot Scarlett walking towards you with her dog Mitzi on the low end of the leash. Which one of the two gets Boris's attention? Whose crotch does he sniff? Scarlett's or Mitzi's?

Why, Mitzi's of course.

The point? Everyone loves dogs. Including dogs.

At this point in my life, I even prefer dogs over kids. I've raised three of the latter over my lifetime while parenting nine dogs, which means I'm a hands-on expert when it comes to being in the company of both. Even at my ripe old age, I still need to have at least two dogs bounding around the house at any given time. But no way in hell would I want even one kid bounding around. Even half a kid would be too much.

Compared with kids, raising a dog is a stroll in the park on a warm summer day. Dogs don't talk back. They don't pout or, if they do, the pout goes away as soon as your hand heads for the treat jar. Dogs are either wagging their tails or tucking them between their legs, which means they have only two moods, sad and happy. Try comparing that to a kid.

My favorite videos on YouTube are those where lost or separated dogs and their owners are reunited. I tear up when the dog spots his long-missed owner, rolls over on his back, then shakes and quakes while his tail pounds the floor like a metronome. I could watch those videos all day.

But I really turn to mush when that dog owner is a soldier returning from some far-off land. Sure, I enjoy watching videos of returning soldiers being reunited with their family, but I'm a basket case when the soldier is being slobbered on by a dog.

My least favorite dog videos? Those ASPCA ads that feature dogs in cages with sad, droopy eyes, dogs that have been mistreated and abused, dogs with their tails cemented between their legs. I assume those videos must work for fundraising purposes or the ASPCA wouldn't employ them, but I fast forward them faster'n you can say, "Don't donate here." I guess this means I'm more moved by happy dogs than sad ones. Same goes with people, by the way.

While dogs work well for people of all ages, they're at their best with us codgers. When we say no, they listen. (Who else in our life does that?) Even after we've said no, they're still madly in love with us as soon as we scratch their ears or rub their tummy. When we hug our dog, we've made its day.

Every dog owner can relate to the following snippet: Let's say you're going out for dinner. Boris's ears are on alert as he watches you dress, fearing the worst. You put on your jacket and grab the car keys and now Boris knows, yes, he's absolutely positive, that you're leaving him behind. Again.

Boris looks up, then his mouth turns down, his tail droops, and his eyes plead for you to stay at home. He's not asking much, he just wants to be around you. A treat on our way out the door helps for an instant. Now if you can just close the door quickly and make a clean getaway. When the door does close, you know that, for Boris, his day is, effective immediately, shot to hell.

Until, that is, you return home. Suddenly, your sins are forgiven, and Boris goes ballistic the moment you open the door. It's like you've just returned from a year in Afghanistan.

Dogs don't purr, but if they did, Boris would start purring as soon as you opened the door. After all, his only goal in life is to be close to you. You're all he's got.

Which is, come to think of it, the reason why I've always pre-ferred dogs over cats. I get more pleasure from a warm tongue than I do from a cold shoulder.

THE WISDOM:

What's not to like about a dog? They come when they're called, they love you unconditionally, and they keep the floor clean of crumbs.

WHY I DON'T EAT FOOD THAT'S GREEN

"Life expectancy would grow by leaps and bounds if vegetables smelled as good as bacon."
—DOUG LARSON

DON'T TELL ANYONE, BUT MY FAVORITE place to eat in Tucson is the Olive Garden. Yes, THAT Olive Garden. No, it isn't because I think their pasta is so fantastic. I have no idea whether it is or isn't, I've never ordered it.

What I do like about the Olive Garden—really, the only reason I eat there—is their house salad. It isn't one of those frou-frou salads with purple-tinged lettuce and sprinkles of unknown substances. Rather it's plain-Jane iceberg lettuce with a couple of other condiments thrown in, like onions, tomatoes, and pepperoncini peppers.

That salad's been on the Olive Garden's menu for at least thirty years. I know this for a fact because Mary and I frequently visited the Olive Garden back in the early 90s. We were living in San Diego at the time and whenever her dad would come to town, we'd head for the Olive Garden. He loved their spaghetti with two meatballs—except that he'd order it with three meatballs, while the menu specified only two. Old age can make you do annoying things.

My friends laugh when I tell them about my fetish for the Olive Garden's salad. The reason they laugh is because I'm famous—within my own tiny world, that is—for not eating vegetables or any other food that is green. I'm not proud of my no-veggie diet, but somehow, it seems to be working. I'm still here.

I'll admit there are certain exceptions to my no-green rule. I'll eat green ice cream if that's the only color left. Green jellybeans go down nicely, too. And then, of course, there's Olive Garden's green salad.

In case you're among the uninitiated, that salad comes with three piping hot, tinged-in-garlic bread sticks. Miraculously, there will still be a third of my salad left along with a couple of breadsticks by the time I push back my chair and call it quits. Chip in a beer to wash it all down and how can you beat a dinner like that for 22 bucks?

Incidentally, I blame this vegetable-free diet of mine on being from Iowa. We Iowans, at least we aging ones, are mostly meat and potato kind of people (probably because our beef is corn fed and comes from our own backyard). My mom is partly to blame, too. When I was a kid, she wouldn't let me leave the dinner table unless I'd eaten all my vegetables. So, once I grew up and left home, I showed her. I quit eating them.

In addition to meat and potatoes, we Iowans are also big fans of corn. OK, so corn is a vegetable, but I eat it anyway, partly because it isn't green. Besides, while corn may be a vegetable to most Americans, to us Iowans it's a staple. Like potatoes are to people from Idaho. Or cheese to those of you from Wisconsin.

I'll admit I feel a tinge of guilt when I'm snacking away on potato chips and ice cream instead of carrots and celery, but I do it anyway. I'm not Catholic, you see, so I manage my guilt well.

I'm not proud of this non-relationship with vegetables. I wish I liked them, I really do. All of my kids are vegetable eaters. My five grandchildren are, too. Which makes me wonder: Why it is that the younger generation eats healthier than we geezers do? I mean, they've inherited our eyes, hair, and a variety of other habits and mannerisms. You'd think they'd have inherited our taste buds, too. Genetics are weird.

While on the topic of healthy foods that I don't eat, I'm reminded of sushi. I'm proud to say I've never had one bite of that vile looking stuff. Mix uncooked fish with green seaweed and add rice cooked in glue, and you can count me out. I'll order a burger instead.

My stance on sushi is nonnegotiable, similar to my stance on Brussels sprouts, broccoli, spinach, and a half dozen other green vegetables that are favorites of the healthy-eater clan.

I'm sorry to say that potato chips and ice cream are not my only regrettable eating habits. I've also never met a Snickers bar I didn't like.

And yet...

I weigh ten pounds less than I did when I graduated from high school. And, despite being almost as old as Betty White, I still play golf at least three times a week and work out on our Pilates reformer daily.

It's probably the sugar that keeps me going.

THE WISDOM:

Diet helps. Exercise helps. Genes help. But flat-out

luck helps the most.

IT TAKES MORE THAN A DREAM

*"Anyone who can take a shower can have a good idea,
what matters is what happens after you towel off."*
—NOLEN BUSHNELL

SOON AFTER MOVING TO BEND, OREGON in 1994, I volunteered
for a business-mentoring organization called SCORE. SCORE is
an acronym for Service Corps of Retired Executives and, while I'd
never been either "retired" or an "executive," somehow, I was qualified to be a SCORE volunteer.

Strangely enough, I soon figured out that I was more qualified
than most "retired executives" since I was a former small business
owner and that's the primary demographic of the people SCORE
serves. No offense to SCORE, but someone who worked for GE
or IBM doesn't have the foggiest idea how a small business's Quick
Books accounting system works.

I totally enjoyed those three years volunteering for SCORE.
Here's a hypothetical story that illustrates the kind of stuff that a
SCORE volunteer gets involved with:

"I have an idea that could be a million-dollar business," Harold
might say, in a tone of voice that suggested he'd just discovered a
cure for cancer."I've figured out how to turn saltwater into beer.
Now all I need to know is how to start and run a brewery."

Harold had been a faithful machinist all his life. He'd been a
dependable and productive employee and was paid a fair wage in

exchange for doing good work. He was also typical of many wannabe entrepreneurs: long on ideas and visions and short on what is needed to turn them into reality.

"I'll be your first customer," I'd reply to Harold, in the spirit of being an early adopter where new beers are concerned.

I'd then dive into the list of questions I'd prepared for people with lofty visions about starting a business. Questions that went like this…

"What do you do now to earn a living?"

"I'm a machinist," Harold would proudly reply.

"Have you ever owned a small business before?"

"No."

"Do you have any idea how much it would cost to build a brewery?"

"A lot, I suppose," he'd reply, eyes downcast.He was beginning to see where my questions were going.

Then I'd begin my standard are-you-sure-you're-ready-to-take-the-risk spiel that I'd perfected over the years. It was designed not so much to squash the wannabe's dreams, but rather to ground him in the reality of what failure will do to both your ego and your financial security.

The thing is, I'd tell people like Harold, owning your own business is the riskiest career of them all. You stand to lose everything, including your IRA, the equity in your house, and your membership in the VFW. Plus, the odds of it succeeding are formidable. Four out of five startups don't survive to celebrate their fifth birthday.

"Being a machinist is an honorable profession," I'd conclude, putting my hand on Harold's shoulder. (These were back in the pre-COVID-19 days). "My advice is to stay with your day job."

Harold then would (hopefully) return to being a machinist, thereby preserving his self-respect along with his savings account.

There was more to those SCORE years than just disparaging people's ideas, however. Check out this true story of Tracey.

"I have this vision for a scented candle business," she began, her jaw set. "I've researched the market and I know my products would fit."

"Tell me more," I replied.

"I've met with the bank and I could qualify for a large enough SBA loan to purchase the equipment I need. I found a light industrial space of 1,500 square feet that would be perfect. Three-year lease, too," she added with a smile. "I don't want too long a lease in the event my company will need to expand."

"I've met with a half dozen potential customers," she continued. "They're ready to order my candles once they're available."

Wow, I thought, Tracey's done her homework."How can I help you?" I asked.

"I have a friend with marketing experience who will help me develop my brand and create a marketing plan. I have another friend, a CPA, who can familiarize me with the financial stuff," she replied. "I need someone with general business experience, someone who's been where I'm going. Would you be willing to mentor me?"

How could I say no?

Thus began a satisfying mentoring relationship. Now I'm in Tucson and Tracey is in Bend so we Zoom once a month: She asks me her usual zinger questions and I do my best to help her come up with the right answers.

Tracey, I should add, went on be the proud owner of a successful, growing business. At the time of this writing, she has fifteen employees and her sales are on a rocket ship trajectory.

For me, there were a lot more Harolds back in those days than there were Traceys, but both of them could use my help. I quickly learned that I could make a difference in their lives.

I could save Harold from trying to be someone he couldn't be.

And I could help Tracey become someone she was meant to be.

THE WISDOM:

It's never about the dream. It's always about the dreamer.

WHAT NOT TO DO WHEN AN EARTHQUAKE GOES OFF IN YOUR HEAD

"All of life is a near-death experience."
—SUNSHINE O'DONNELL

IT'S JANUARY 2020. MARY AND I are living in Tucson now, but I'm back in Bend, visiting for the week. Bend has been pummeled by snow for three straight days; Mt. Bachelor, its beloved ski mountain, has been dumped on with more than 100 inches of fresh powder. The local skiers and snowboarders are giddy. Large quantities of snow make some people happy. I'm not one of them.

I return to Bend once a month because I love the community and because I need to catch up on some of the stuff I'm still involved in. I'm staying in the house we built 20 years ago, which is now up for sale. The house appears to be lonely and forlorn, as if it's feeling sad because there's no one around to enjoy it. It's known happier times.

By Friday night I've finished my week's work and am scheduled to catch a flight to Tucson at 11am the following morning. I'm over-tired from a long week and sleep is not cooperating. It's 2am and I'm in that nether stage where you're not sure whether you're awake or asleep. Suddenly, something shakes violently inside my head, as if my brain has just shifted to a new location. The violence is accompanied by a cracking sound that lasts for only a second or two. And then, quicker than it came, it's gone. The bedroom is deathly quiet.

If I wasn't sure whether I was asleep or awake before, I'm sure now. I'm bug-eyed, wondering what in the hell just happened to me. Since I'm alone, there's no one to talk to, no one to help me figure out what I just felt. So I remain where I am, in bed, on my back, staring at the ceiling. I'm afraid to move for fear something in my head will rattle or fall out.

Finally, I decide to get up. I slowly swing my legs from under the covers to the floor. On cue, my head begins to spin. I try to stand but the room twirls. I'm dizzy and lightheaded, which isn't surprising since an earthquake just went off in my head. I lay back down and reach for my iPad on the nightstand. I'll see if Google can help me figure things out.

My vision is blurry. I can read the word "Google" on the iPad home page, but I can't make out the smaller print. I put the iPad back on the nightstand and lay my head back on the pillow. It's 2:30 in the morning. My plane leaves for Tucson in less than nine hours.

I think of calling Mary but what good would that do? It's 2:30 in Tucson, too, and she wouldn't hear her cell phone ring; she charges it in the kitchen.

I have three choices. I can either call 9-1-1, try and make it to the garage and drive myself to the ER, or see if I can go back to sleep. I choose the third option and somehow, miracle of miracles, I fall asleep.

I couldn't sleep before the earthquake struck but now I can. What's up with that?

I wake at 7am and my balance and vision problems are gone. After checking in with Mary, at her suggestion I call my friend Mark, a recently retired ER doc who lives nearby. I ask if he could stop by and help me figure out what just happened.

"Jim," he says an hour later, following a 15-minute barrage of doc-type questions. "You just had a TIA."

"Wow, I've always wanted one of those," I say, my mind shifting into its dark mode. "And just exactly what is a TIA?"

"TIA stands for transient ischemic attack," he replies, in doctor-like fashion. "It's a brief interruption of blood flow to the brain that causes temporary stroke-like symptoms."

"So, what should I do?" I ask. "My plane leaves at eleven o'clock."

"I suggest you go to the ER here in Bend. They need to take tests and determine the extent of the damage."

"But I'd miss my plane."

"You can catch another one later, if the ER gives you a green light."

Well, Mark doesn't know me *that* well. I want to get the hell home. This instant. I want to be where it's warm and sunny and where Mary and I can talk this earthquake thing through. So, I catch the 11am plane despite Mark's sage advice and I'm home in one piece by 7pm that evening.

Over the next few weeks, I take a variety of heart and head tests, answer lots of doc-type questions, and life goes happily on.

Several weeks following my brain quake, I play golf with Bob, a frequent golfing buddy in Tucson. He's a doc, too. (It's advisable to have as many doc friends as you can when you get to be my age.) We share a golf cart that day.

"Jim," he says between forgettable shots. "You took a big chance by catching that plane instead of going to the ER."

"I wanted to get home," I reply, repeating what I'd said to Mary and also to my doc here in Tucson, along with a few other well-intentioned friends who wondered about my choice of options.

"But you could have…"

"Could have what? Croaked?"

"Well, yeah."

"Bob," I reply. "I suppose I would have inconvenienced a few folks on the plane if I'd croaked on the flight, but my time is gonna come sooner or later. If it's on a Delta flight from Bend to Tucson, then so be it."

"But you could have…"

"I'm well into my bonus years now," I interrupt, overriding Bob's well-intentioned attempt to tell me that I'd made a lousy choice. "My life's in order, I don't have a bucket list, and I've paid my rent to be here on this earth. I'm OK with whatever happens next."

"In fact," I say, as I watch the golf ball I just struck soar into the bushes and brambles. "In a macabre kind of way, I'm kinda looking forward to whatever's next."

"Who knows," I conclude, dropping another ball where the last one disappeared.

"Maybe what's next could be even better than what's now."

THE WISDOM:

The question is not how to avoid death but, rather,

how to prepare for it when it arrives.

FORGET THAT COLONOSCOPY AND CANCEL THAT BYPASS SURGERY

"Sometimes the remedy is worse than the disease."
—FRANCIS BACON

DR. EZEKIEL EMANUEL, IN THE OCTOBER 2014 issue of *Atlantic* magazine, raised more than a few eyebrows with a thoughtful piece entitled "Why I Hope to Die at 75." The premise of his article, written when Dr. Emanuel was 57, was that he will have led a complete life by the time he's 75 and that living too long would be a "loss" (his word). "Aging takes its inevitable toll," the good doctor went on, "and renders many of us, if not disabled, then faltering and declining, a state that may not be worse than death, but is nonetheless deprived."

"Age 75," Dr. Emanuel thus concluded, "is a pretty good age to stop."

Dr. Emanuel is no slouch. He's a nationally recognized oncologist with a long resume of involvement on the national medical scene. His article generated months of feedback from *Atlantic*'s readers, most opposed to some, if not all, of his message. I was 77 when I first read it and found it thought provoking but not relevant. 75 was in my rearview mirror and had been a good year for me, as was 76. 77 was on its way to being just as good as the prior two.

Emanuel went on to explain that he's not going to do anything drastic at age 75—or any age—to put an end to his life. (He's adamantly opposed to euthanasia and physician-assisted suicide.) Rather, it's his approach to health care that will do a 180; he'll no longer do anything to medically prolong his life. No more colonoscopies, no pacemakers, no bypass surgeries. Even flu shots are out, the good doctor says. (This was pre-COVID-19; I'll bet he got vaccinated.)

Pneumonia, Emanuel added in a related aside, is a friend of the aged. It can save us all from the "cold gradations of decay." Which begs the question: Will pneumonia pills be available at our local pharmacy anytime soon? It'd sure beat the hell out of laying around for a week in hospice.

Dr. Emanuel goes on to say that for most of us (outliers excepted), living past 75 is not in our best interest, especially if we have Alzheimer's or are survivors of a major stroke. I'm sure I skipped over his reference to a stroke when I originally read the piece, but it grabbed my attention when I reread it now.

Today, at age 84 (I'm an outlier in Dr. Emanuel's eyes), I'm even more at odds with his exit-at-75 message than I was when I originally read it. I'm still—knock on wood—actively involved and don't intend to hang it up anytime soon. I recently reread and digested Emanuel's article, and then Mary and I invited Bob, my doctor friend, along with his wife Ettie, to dinner at our favorite Italian restaurant. Bob is 72 and still goes to the office four days a week. In Dr. Emanuel's eyes, he's on the fringe of being an outlier, too.

Our ad hoc Pasta Panel agreed that by the time 2030 rolls around and Dr. Emanuel is 73, his opinions may well have changed. We believe he's flat out wrong on the number 75. Remember, I'm 84 and Bob is 72, which makes us semi-experts on the topic of old age. Biased experts, perhaps, and not as well read on the topic as Dr. Emanuel, but we're living those years and he isn't. Or hasn't.

Our Pasta Panel further agreed that, in lieu of 75, there should be a certain age when one's outlook on health care should change. Sure, that certain age could be 75, but it could also be 65 or 85, depending upon the health and wellbeing of the body involved.

Everything that's done medically should be done with the goal of maintaining a person's comfort and dignity, Dr. Bob opined. Just keep us warm, hydrated, and do whatever needs to be done to control the pain. And, most of all, prepare us mentally to let go.

Recovery as a goal? Not so much. Or not at all, depending upon the situation. On that conclusion, the Pasta Panel agreed with Dr. Emanuel—when the handwriting is on the wall, a revision of the kind of treatment the patient gets makes sense. The current system of dragging one's life out is inhumane. We treat our dogs better.

My recent TIA experience made Emanuel's thoughts on the topic of health care more relevant. When, and if, my major stroke comes along, I'd prefer not to be a survivor. But if I am, I don't want to survive for long. I want to be all here, not half here. I've never been good at fractions.

For me, my TIA was a message that, at 84, I've now reached that "certain age." It's time to change my philosophy about healthcare and put Dr. Emanuel's credo to work. From now on my doctor visits will focus on comfort and dignity, and less on recovery.

To my mind, Dr. Emanuel's hypothesis is right. He just got the number wrong.

THE WISDOM:

Be grateful for what you have, be thankful for

what you've accomplished, and be prepared for

when it's all over.

IN PREPARATION FOR WHEN YOUR LIGHTS GO OUT

"I am not afraid to die, I just don't want to be there when it happens."—WOODY ALLEN

AT AGE 84, I'M ONE OF the lucky ones. Since the average lifespan of the white American male is 79, I've got five bonus years of elderhood under my belt. Five years that two of my three best friends growing up didn't get. The odds caught up with them, while sparing me.

My dad's heart gave out at age 64, so it sure wasn't *his* genes that got me this far. Mom's genes may have helped, but she died in an automobile accident at age 79, so we'll never know what she brought to the longevity table.

One of those two best friends played professional football after college, followed by 35 years of lawyering, which he was actively doing right up to the day he was diagnosed with brain cancer. Both of his parents had lived until their mid-90s so he had all kinds of friendly genes going for him. No matter; at 79, his luck ran out.

Meanwhile here I am, wobbly but still standing. With a few minor health-related exceptions, I'm enjoying my bonus years. Similar to most people my age, I have my share of aches and pains, but not enough to complain about. Besides, who'd listen?

"All you can do is the best you can do," someone once said, and I've done the best I can do, given the cards I've been dealt. Sure, I've had a few major stumbles along the way. I was a good father but not a great one because I loved my work too much. And I failed my oldest son and will regret that for as long as I live. I didn't do the best I could do for him.

In addition to potato chips and ice cream, I also love chocolate and Pepsi, if you count that as a stumble. Some do. For me, they're worth the downsides.

I'm hopeful that Mary would say I've done the best I can do as a husband and best friend. Yes, I've forgotten an anniversary now and then, and when something needed fixing around the house, she's had to fix it. I must have stood in the wrong line when handiness was doled out.

But Mary had been a consenting adult when she'd said "yes." We'd been friends for many years before we married; she knew damn well what she was getting into. We're still best friends, although I'm sure she sometimes wonders why.

It's been said that life is too short. That certainly applies to dogs and cats, but not necessarily to humans. For me, I'll be happy if I'm still around when I'm 90 and have a decent quality of life. No quality of life? Thanks but no thanks. You can count me out.

One hundred years old is too many and 75 not enough, which makes 90 a logical compromise. Right now, on this sunny day in February 2021, I'm satisfied right where I am. 84 is old, but not *too* old. Ninety still sounds good.

Whenever my lights do start to dim, I'll be ready, I'm fascinated by whatever's coming next. Steve Jobs, one of the more famous Americans who checked out before his time, had a glimpse of what's next when it was his time to move on. "Oh wow, oh wow, oh wow," Jobs said to his wife on his deathbed, as if he were seeing something new, something exciting.

Something that would get his adrenaline running again.

THE WISDOM:

We wake up thousands of mornings over our

lifetimes and then one morning we don't.

Thousands of good ones and then one bad one?

Sounds like a fair trade to me.

PART TWO

The Wisdom We Learn
from People

"In life, it's not where you go, it's who you travel with." —CHARLES SCHULZ

I WONDER IF STEVE JOBS KNEW WHAT HE WAS DOING TO US WHEN HE INVENTED THE CELL PHONE?

"I'm having people over to stare at their phones later, if you want to come by."—ANONYMOUS

IT WAS A WEEK OR SO before Christmas, which meant it was time to do a phone check-in with my sister Chris. She lives in Denver.

"Hi there," she said, answering my ring. "Merry-almost-Christmas." Scrape. Pant.

"Backatcha," I replied. Her voice sounded weird, as if she'd been running. Which is doubtful. She's 78.

"To what do I owe the pleasure of this call?" she asked.

Scrape. Pant.

"I just wanted to officially wish you a Merry Christmas," I replied. "Hey, what's that noise in the background? Are you alright?"

"Oh, that. Yeah, I'm shoveling snow," she replied. "You're probably hearing my shovel scrape. We got six inches last night."

"So, let me guess, you're out of breath from shoveling, right? I'm hearing a panting sound, too."

"How discerning of you, James," Chris replied. She has a sarcastic streak that comes from being a little sister. We all know how little sisters can be.

"But…but…how can you talk on the phone and shovel snow at the same time?" I asked. "Last I heard, shoveling required two hands."

"Oh, that. Well, my phone's hooked to my bra and it's also blue-toothed to my hearing aids," she said, laughing. "Look, no hands." Sarcastic *and* smartass.

For me, shoveling snow used to be a time to commune with nature, reflect on life, and ponder the wonder of the universe, all the while gazing in amazement as those dainty little snowflakes spiraled softly to the ground. And then piled up. And up.

They'll be no communing with nature anymore, at least for people like Chris. Shoveling snow has turned into yet another opportunity to gab on the cell phone, in lieu of communing, reflecting, pondering, and all such other remnants of days gone by.

I shouldn't be surprised at Chris choosing not to commune with nature while shoveling snow. Thanks to my cell phone, I've also chosen—on too many occasions—*not* to commune myself.

Take, for instance, my visits to what was my favorite Bend neighborhood pub, the Phoenix. Whenever Mary was out of town, I'd make a beeline for the Phoenix, Bend's version of Boston's *Cheers*. I knew all the bartenders there, most of the waitresses, and quite a few of the regulars. In the universe of the *Cheers* sitcom, I was Norm, happily rooted at the end of the bar where I could solve the problems of the world while sipping my one-and-only beer of the night.

Unlike Norm, alcohol is not my friend. One beer's enough.

There'd be a whole lot of communing going on at the Phoenix while I was there—people bullshitting with friends, chatting up with a stranger or catching up on the latest sports news from the bartenders. Such friendly communing is, after all, the primary reason God created pubs in the first place.

So what would I do too often while perched at the Phoenix? Why, I'd haul out Jobs' four-ounce Apple doodad and start scrolling. Local news. Worldwide news. Tomorrow's weather. You name it, and I needed to know it.

And then, when I was sure no one was looking, I'd check in on Facebook.

OK, so I'll admit it, even though I'm an old guy, I'm never—yes, never—without my phone. I'm hooked on the damn thing. I can use it for dialing 911 when I have a TIA, I can use it to get where I'm going without getting lost, and I can use it to call Mary when I can't remember what I'm supposed to pick up at the grocery store.

I'm hooked on that phone just like my grandkids are, except that my reasons are different. I doubt if they have 911 on speed dial.

So, yes, I'm an addict. You'll never see me without my cell phone. And yet...

I've seen way too many YouTube videos of people walking into inanimate objects while staring at their cell phone. I've sat in way too many meetings watching folks sneak peeks at their phone when they oughta be listening to what's being said. I've had way too many near-death experiences (well, one, which was way too many) thanks to a teenage girl texting while driving. She cost me a year of my life.

Somewhere between the benefits and drawbacks of cell phones lies a tipping point. A point where the phone transitions from being useful and enjoyable to being compelling and demanding. A point where reaching for your cell phone becomes a reflex action, whether it's ringing or buzzing or just plain waiting. A point where having a cell phone in your hand is similar to what used to be having a binky in your mouth.

Nothing to do? Hand goes to back pocket. Out comes cell phone. Fits neatly in palm of hand. Feels reassuring. Planets are aligned. Life is good.

Sound familiar?

Haven't you wondered whether or not Steve Jobs knew, or at least suspected, what his invention would do to its users?

Don't you also wonder if he envisioned an item of woman's underwear doubling as a cell tower?

What a rich imagination that guy must have had.

THE WISDOM:

There's a time and a place for cell phones. The problem is, there are too many times and places.

YES, THERE ARE KIDS WHO KNOW EXACTLY WHAT THEY WANT TO BE WHEN THEY GROW UP

"If you don't love what you do, you won't do it with much passion and conviction."—MIA HAMM, OLYMPIC GOLD MEDAL WINNER

SEVERAL WEEKS AGO, I STOPPED BY my bank in Bend to deposit a check.The teller was a girl who looked like she was fresh out of high school. The nameplate on the counter said her name was Kelly.

"How's your day going, Kelly?"I asked. Uh-oh, here I go again. Why can't I just do my business and move on?

"It's been interesting," she replied, shaking her head. "I just helped a husband and wife who must have got up on the wrong side of the bed. I did my best to make them happy, but it wasn't good enough." I knew what she was talking about. For a few long months back in the early 1960s I did a stint as a bank teller. We gotta start somewhere.

"Are you from Bend?" I asked Kelly. This isn't as stupid a question as it might seem. Most Bendites come from somewhere else.

"No, I'm from Silver Lake," she replied. "My family has a ranch over there." At the mention of her family, her smile stretched to her ears. "We run about three hundred head of cattle."

Silver Lake is a dot on the map located deep in the boondocks of Oregon, an hour and a half southeast of Bend in windswept high-desert country. The unincorporated community consists of a gas station, a small store, and, at last count, 76 residents. Not to mention large quantities of mule deer, antelope, elk, coyotes, eagles, and, of course, Silver Lake's number one commercial crop: cattle.

Silver Lake is also the home of the famous Cowboy Dinner Tree restaurant. Mary and I made the hour and a half drive from Bend to have dinner there many years ago.

The Cowboy Dinner Tree owners weren't kidding when they dubbed it a cowboy restaurant. Until a couple of years ago everything was cooked over a roaring fire. (There was no electricity in the vicinity). You waited for your reservation in a teepee in front of the restaurant and the steaks were the size of a baseball glove. The only other item on the menu other than steaks was a chicken. Not just a breast or a thigh, mind you, but a whole damn chicken.

You'd better be hungry, buckaroo, when you visit the Cowboy Dinner Tree.

"How many siblings do you have?" I asked Kelly. I was on a roll now.

"Just one brother," she said. "He's in the Army and just deployed to Poland."

"And is banking your chosen profession?"

"No," she laughed. "I'm here because there aren't any jobs in Silver Lake. I'm waiting for my parents to retire."

"Oh, so you're going to take over the family ranch?"

"Yes, my brother and I are. As soon as he's discharged." Cue the million dollar smile again.

Kelly's a member-in-good-standing of Generation Z. I don't know what the statistics say for Zs, but their predecessors, the Millennials, are forecast to have eleven different jobs before they retire. I suspect Zs are somewhere in the same ballpark.

Yet here Kelly was, right out of high school, already knowing what her chosen career was going to be. The one and only career she'd (presumably) be pursuing until the day it was her turn to cede the family ranch to *her* kids.

Wouldn't we all have loved to know what our career would be immediately upon graduating from high school? Heck, Kelly probably already knew she'd be a rancher when she was in grade school and has been preparing for the job ever since, learning how to bale hay, brand calves, and care for horses. Talk about an in-house training program.

Kelly and her brother will also have their own built-in mentors and support group when they take over the business: their parents. With her brother as co-owner, she'll have an equally trained partner and someone she can unreservedly trust. She'll join the millions of Americans, past and present, who have started and finished their working life on a ranch or a farm.

I'm eternally jealous of people like Kelly. She won't have to spend 16 years of her life (like I did) searching for a career she can love. She already knows she is going to love her career before she even begins it. Now, all she has to do is learn how to make a living at it.

I didn't mention this to Kelly but, as with most career paths, there's a downside to her choice. There are 100,000 fewer small farms and ranches in the U.S. today than there were eight years ago. Government policies are the primary culprit, or so say the people who are—or were—in the ranching business.

I'm sure this downside isn't news to Kelly. She, her brother, and her parents must have had this discussion more than once. I'd bet she can tell you how her ranch is going to buck the trend. I wanted to ask that question next but the line behind me was piling up.

Similar to any other path young people choose to follow, there's no guarantee that Kelly's career choice is going to be successful.

But there *is* a guarantee she'll love what she does.

THE WISDOM:

Once you love what you do, you'll never have to

work again.

WOMEN BOND WHILE MEN MAKE FRIENDS

"Maybe our girlfriends are our soul mates and guys are just people to have fun with."—CANDACE BUSHNELL

IT'S LATE MARCH IN 2020 AND another ho-hum sunny day in Tucson, which is a good part of the reason we decided to relocate here. COVID-19 is in its early days and Mary and I are dutifully minding the rules and quarantining. I'm pounding away contentedly at my keyboard when Mary walks into my office and plops down on the couch. Her eyes are glassy.

"Uh-oh," I said. "What happened?"

"I'm in shock," she replied. "When I was in high school, we had a group of eight girls who were tight friends. We played sports together, chased boys together, and did all the wild and crazy stuff that high school girls do. That was 50 years ago. I haven't heard boo from any of them since we graduated and went our separate ways." She paused, her eyes clouding.

"Thirty minutes ago, I received an email from Emily, one of the eight, addressed to the other seven of us." Mary then went on to explain what the email was about, which made little sense to me, but hey, I'm a guy so what would I know.

"Jim, within an hour the emails were flying between the eight of us. It's as if nothing had changed over those 50 years. Today could just as well be 1970, sans email and computers. I...I...I can't describe how nostalgic that makes me feel."

Well, Mary's high school days may have been the first time she bonded with a group of females but, as it turned out, it would not be the last. Way back in 1998—we were living in Bend at the time—seven women and Mary ended up sitting at the same table following a women's golf tournament. Some were already friends, but several were strangers. As the evening progressed, idle chatting morphed into intense bonding, which then turned into future event planning. While alcohol may have been a factor that evening, the bonding of those women would turn out to withstand the test of time.

Over the next 22 years, that pack of subsequently-reduced-to-seven women partied together, traveled together, and bonded together, as tightly as any group of women possibly could. They called themselves the BAGG ladies (Bend Area Golf Girls) and today the texts, emails, and Zooms can erupt at the slightest provocation.

Fast forward to early 2020. Mary and I had sold our Bend home of twenty-five years and relocated permanently to Tucson. Once situated, we joined a local golf club made up largely of Midwestern and Pacific Northwest expats, which meant that the club's culture made us feel right at home.

A few months after relocating and mixing with the locals, Mary had once again bonded with another group of like-minded women—eight friends who, similar to the BAGGs, play golf together, plan social events together, and exchange endless emails, texts, and Zooms. This latest group has dubbed themselves the GNO (Girls Night Out) girls, which is what they were doing once a month before COVID-19 came along. For Mary, the GNO group was, as Yogi Berra once said, déjà vu all over again.

After Mary had finished telling me about the call with her high school friends, she turned to me and said, "You know, Jim, I must be some sort of a pack woman. It seems I've always needed a group of girlfriends to bond with."

She was right, of course; most women I know enjoy traveling in a pack, especially when compared to us guys. While I also had a wide collection of men-friends while we were living in Bend, we didn't Zoom, trade emails, or share intimate secrets. Instead, when not working or recreating, we'd retreat to our man caves or plop down on our Barcaloungers and watch a ball game. No hardcore bonding for us.

While I can't speak for all men, I'd rather be pounding away at my keyboard or pulling up sports reruns or Ted Talks on You Tube than Zooming and giggling with a bunch of guys. Sure, I enjoy sharing a beer or playing golf with my buddies, but they'll be no running in packs for me. A good dose of male companionship is necessary now and then, but I don't need the deep bonding experiences that Mary and her friends seem to crave.

Can women and men be *that* much different?

What a stupid question, why, of course they can. What a boring world this would be if the two genders were the same.

While I may have had more friends than Mary did in Bend, she had (and still has) more *close* friends. In the old days when my friends and I *would* get together, we'd talk about sports, politics, or sex; today such banter is mostly about sports and health. Politics aren't fun to talk about anymore and we've forgotten most of what we knew about sex.

While I'm content with the new guy friends I've made in Tucson and don't need any more, Mary is busily gobbling up new chums at the same time she's bonding with her old ones back in Bend.

In her world, "bonding" isn't just about chatting and exchanging texts and emails. Rather, it goes deeper than that, including things that men would never do, like giggle and hug.

And, when the discussions go deep, cry.

THE WISDOM:

We all need friends. Women just need theirs at a deeper level.

WHEN YOUR BUSINESS SUFFERS AND ONLY FACEBOOK KNOWS WHY

"There's life without Facebook? Really, send me the link."—ANONYMOUS

WHEN I FIRST MET SHANNON IN 2014, she was running a small but growing Bend nonprofit that manufactured and sold a line of women's loungewear. The loungewear was sewn in India, then warehoused and sold in the United States. That nonprofit had been on a rocket ship trajectory since she founded it; sales had doubled each year and were on a path to double again. Shannon, she of boundless charisma and inexhaustible passion, was its founder and CEO.

At the height of her nonprofit's growth, Shannon converted it to a "B Corporation." B Corps are for-profit businesses that have a social impact mission: they do well at the same time they're doing good.

Along with her charisma and passion, Shannon is also armed with one other irresistible weapon: a smile as wide as the Columbia River. Furthermore, she's not afraid to use it.

A friend introduced us. Over a cup of coffee at a local coffee shop, she put her elbows on the table and flashed that smile.

"Jim," she began, "I'm committed to growing my business to $250 million in sales over the next ten years."

"That's a lot of jobs you'd be creating," I replied, my business hat on.

"It is, but we'll be doing much more than creating jobs," she replied, her face turning crimson as the passion kicked in. "Rather, we'll be changing lives."

"Our employees aren't the kind of people you're thinking about," she continued, her eyes glistening. "They're all women. Young women. Even girls. Many with children and all without a husband." She paused for effect.

"Our employees live in India, Jim, and were sex trade workers before they became seamstresses. Our mission is to take them off the streets. To give them a job worth working and a life worth living."

The smile was doing its job as she wrapped up her story."Jim, we're providing hope and opportunity through living-wage jobs, skills training, and education." Bingo, that did it. I agreed to get involved and together we formed an Advisory Board.

Shannon is as captivated by her organization's mission as anyone I've met over my sixty years of being involved in small businesses and nonprofits.If *Guinness World Records* had a passion category for founders of social impact organizations, she'd be at the top of the list.

Her vision took root when she and her husband, Jeff, vacationed in India in 2010. Once there, they set out to learn what made that nation tick. One of the many sights they saw as they strolled the streets of Bombay was the proliferation of young women and girls in the sex trade.

What she saw made her angry. Shortly after returning to the States, she shucked off a successful corporate career and set out to do something about what she'd just seen. She founded Sudara— Indian Sanskrit for "beautiful"—as a 501 (c) 3 nonprofit. Sudara sold most of its loungewear in the U.S. using Facebook's ad platform and recirculating any profits back into the business.

Up and up Sudara's sales went in its early years: $500,000, the first year, $1 million the next, $2 million the third. Four million was right around the corner, when Shannon relocated her business and its warehouse from California to Bend.

Everyone was a winner back in those exciting days: Shannon, her customers, the seamstresses in India, and, of course, the quiet giant lurking silently in the background, her sales and marketing partner, Facebook. Facebook provided the platform that offered the outreach that Sudara needed to reach its community of far-flung customers. Shannon's formula for success was locked in. Nothing could go wrong.

Except that it did. Without warning, Facebook changed its algorithm. Whereupon Sudara's sales plummeted and so did its profitability. Only the Facebook engineers knew how it was done and only their bosses know why it was done.

In one of the many ways that technology can shortchange the people who depend on it, Facebook neglected to tell Shannon, and (presumably) its other two million small business marketing partners, that they were changing that algorithm. Transparency is fleeting in the world of technology; what you see is not always what you get. And what you get is not always in your best interest.

As one might expect, Shannon was incapable of throwing in the towel as her sales fell. Over the next year or so, between struggles to pay Sudara's bills and make payroll, she pivoted her business model from being dependent on Facebook to working digitally within her own customer base. Today, Sudara lives on, but Shannon's lofty ten-year expectations have taken a serious hit.

So goes the life of a social entrepreneur, which Shannon most certainly is. The committed ones and the persevering ones will recover and move on—and Shannon's one of the committed and persevering ones. She'll be around when others would have thrown in the towel.

Today, thanks to Zoom, I meet with Shannon semi-regularly. I still get to see that dazzling smile.

We're also Facebook friends, but she never posts anymore.

The giant giveth and the giant taketh away.

THE WISDOM:

There are three things in life over which we have no control: the weather, taxes, and Facebook.

YOU NAME IT AND I'VE QUIT IT

"I don't care to belong to a club that accepts people like me as its members."—GROUCHO MARX

MARY IS ALWAYS PREPARING FOR SOMETHING. The further away that something is, the more prepared she gets. Guests for dinner on Saturday night? The table is set by Friday afternoon. A trip to Boston in November? We have our plane tickets by September. Me leaving the house to play golf? She's standing in the doorway with my sunglasses, billfold, and car keys. I always forget at least one of them.

I was reminded of how prepared she can be several weeks ago after we'd sold our Bend house in preparation for our move to Tucson. We were scheduled to move out by March 15. Naturally, she had things organized and ready to go by mid-February.

"Did you know I once was once a Cub Scout?" I asked her as we were talking about preparing for the move. Yes, I'm a master at asking seemingly irrelevant questions out of the blue.

Well, that question may appear to be irrelevant to the casual observer, but it made perfect sense to me: You see, the Cub Scout motto is to "Be Prepared" and, like I said, Mary is always prepared. So, this in turn, led to me remember the Cub Scout motto. The working of man's mind is a scary thing.

"No, I didn't know you were a Cub Scout," she said, rolling her eyes. She's used to my irrelevant questions. "And just how long did your involvement in the Cub Scouts last?"

I should have known that question was coming. "Less than a year," I mumbled, studying my shoes.

"That's about how long you lasted in your college fraternity too, right?"

"Well, yeah, I guess." Actually, it was six months.

Sometimes I wish she wouldn't remember every little thing I tell her.

When it comes to joining and unjoining organizations, I'm likely near the top of the list of the World's Extraordinary Quitters. I joined one of Bend's Rotary Clubs twenty years ago and that lasted less than a month. My reason for quitting? Rotary clubs meet once every week, 52 times a year. I'd have a hard time meeting with Nicole Kidman that often. Besides, I'm incapable of doing the same thing, seeing the same people, pledging the same allegiance, over and over again.

Dependable? Hmm, not so much, one might say. You wouldn't want me on your Wednesday night bowling team.

I was also a Jaycee for a several months when I lived in Moline, Illinois, but I unjoined them too. It was too cold and miserable in December to be standing outside selling Christmas trees. If I have to be selling something to be a member, you can count me out. Especially in subzero weather.

When you think about it, I guess I'm actually very good at joining things. I'm just not so good at staying with the things I join. As a result, I've become proficient at quitting. Practice makes perfect, they say.

I know what you're thinking: I must be antisocial. I don't like people. I don't work well with people. Or people don't like me.

None of the above is true. Well, with the possible exception of the last one.

Now don't get me wrong, I can be a dependable, responsible, contributing member of an organization. As long, that is—and here's the punch line—as the organization I belong to is mine. Or, at least, as long as I'm in charge. For better or for worse, it has to be a business or organization where I can make the game-breaking decisions.

In short—cue an apologetic sigh here—I need to be the boss.

In some ways, I'd like to change this behavioral quirk of mine; it's an intractable trait and one I'm not proud of. But we're all born with an inventory of related characteristics that drive our behavior and make us who we are. Some of us like to eat at the Olive Garden, some of us will only drive Jeeps, and some of us can't remember doctor's appointments. You've got your own list.

So yes, one of my behavioral quirks is that I need to be in charge of whatever it is I'm doing, which makes me a lousy follower and a just-as-lousy employee. I learned this about myself when I was in the Air Force, and I learned it again from the two jobs I had before I bought my first business. It's no fun to be lousy at your job.

It's not just me who has this need-to-be-in-charge quirk. There are people out there who need to lead in every sector within our community and country: government, education, nonprofit, faith-based, and business. My sector just happens to be business, small business, that is.

That's where I'm the happiest.

That's where I can do the most good.

That's where I belong.

THE WISDOM:

The buck has to stop on someone's desk. It may as

well be yours.

A MIDLIFE CRISIS ISN'T ALWAYS A CRISIS

"I'm due to have my mid-life crisis and you're invited. Doors open at 8am."—UNKNOWN

WIKIPEDIA INFORMS US THAT THE MIDLIFE crisis phenomenon is "a psychological crisis brought about by events that highlight a person's growing age, inevitable mortality, and possibly lack of accomplishments in life." A person's midlife crisis can, *Wikipedia* continues, "produce feelings of intense depression, remorse, and high levels of anxiety."

Sheesh, that sure sounds more like a midlife death sentence to me. I went through something that resembles what most people would identify as a midlife crisis and I don't regret it one bit. I'd do it over again. My son Todd would say the same thing. We both went through a midlife something-or-other between the ages of 45 and 60. But "crisis" was not a word either of us would use to describe it.

In Todd's case, his midlife something-or-other began when, at age 50, he bought a Jeep. Not just any Jeep, mind you, but one of those lumbering, open-air vehicles that you drive down the street with the wind rushing through your hair…and through everything else.His wife, Robin, was okay with the decision. "Better a Jeep than a Porsche," she shrugged.

Eight years later, he still owns that Jeep but drives it maybe a half-dozen times a year. Otherwise, it rests placidly in his garage, biding its time. Personally, I think he was making a statement when he bought it. "I want to feel young again," he was saying, or something to that effect. Haven't we all had that thought at one time or another?

That's not all Todd did around the time he turned 50. He also started hiking. I mean hardcore, long-distance hiking, in some cases involving mountains: He climbed all of New England's 50 tallest peaks; Tanzania's Kilimanjaro; and Argentina's Acononcagua—South America's highest peak at 23,000 feet. Such extreme hiking, in conjunction with a physical fitness kick, was an integral part of what was happening to him at the period of time.

"Just adding a new twist to my life," he once said, in between planning his next forays. If adding a new twist to one's life is a "crisis," then I'll be playing in the NBA next year.

As for me, my new twist included a divorce, a divorce that, it should be noted, ultimately turned out to be best for both parties. Several years later, that divorce was followed by what amounted to another divorce: I sold my fourth and final Minneapolis company. That sale set Mary and me free to leave Minneapolis and head west to San Diego and then on to Bend, where I'd start a new career and Mary would, after years of working for someone else, start a new career too. She bought a small business herself. She and that business would flourish for the next twenty-five years.

If Todd's and my experiences are labeled "crises," I say bring 'em on.

A better word for what Todd and I went through would be "transitions," as in the two of us transitioned from one stage to another. *Dictionary.com* defines the word "transition" as a "movement, passage, or change from one position, state, stage, subject, concept, etc., to another."

Once Todd's kids were grown and out of the house, he chose to *transition* the way he'd spend his time away from work. Instead of attending his kid's softball and hockey games, he transitioned to hiking. My ex-wife and I transitioned from being married to one another to being married to someone else. The dynamics of marriage change with age, sometimes for the better, sometimes for the worse. In this case it was for the better. For both of us.

For sure, my transition was more dramatic than Todd's as well as being more stressful. Still, it did not come even close to "producing feelings of intense depression, remorse, and high levels of anxiety." Low levels of anxiety perhaps, but zero depression and zero remorse. I think I can say the same for my ex.

I'm not saying there's no such thing as a midlife crisis. I've known more than a few folks who have labored through one. But in all their cases, their experiences *were* accompanied by varying degrees of depression and remorse. And in most cases, their futures were negatively impacted.

Certainly, the midlife crisis as described by *Wikipedia* is, in fact, a crisis. Fortunately, most of us won't be experiencing one, at least if you define it the way *Wikipedia* does—or if you define it the way the inventor of the term did. Elliott Jaques was a 48-year-old Canadian who originally published his theory in 1965 in *The International Journal of Psychoanalysis.* The title of the article? "Death and the Mid-life Crisis."

Death? Yikes, a consideration of death wasn't part of Todd's decision to buy a Jeep or hike mountains. And it was only tangentially part of our divorce decision, when my ex and I asked ourselves if we were currently living with the person with whom we wanted to share the second half of our lives.

There are plenty of other transitions that most of us will experience over the course of our lifetimes; Todd's and mine just happened to take place in midlife. There will also be transitions at any stage and they can be driven by a change in employment, locale, health, or the number of dependents we have sharing our home.

Transitions can happen when we least expect them or when we most need them. They know no calendar.

They only know when it's time for a change.

THE WISDOM:

How we navigate life's transitions will be determined by who we are. The outcome of those transitions will determine who we become.

LEARNING FROM THOSE YOU TEACH

"A textbook can teach you the principles of biology, but a mentor can show you how to think like a biologist."
—DAVID BROOKS

FOR THOSE OF US WHO ARE looking for ways to dull the onset of old age while, at the same time, helping others improve their life, I know of one double-whammy technique that's designed to do both. That technique is based partially on the premise that, for us older folks, being around younger folks can be an enjoyable, invigorating, and inspiring experience. Not to mention educational.

The technique I'm talking about? Why, of course, it's mentoring.

Today's typical mentors are boomers along with my silent generation peers, while our typical mentees are GenXers, Millennials, and, most recently, the youngest kids on the block, GenZs. There's no rule, however, that says the GenXers, Millennials, and GenZs can't mentor people younger than themselves as well. There are no age boundaries where mentoring is concerned; a ten-year-old can mentor a five-year old, a 90-year-old can mentor an 80-year-old. Anyone can mentor anyone.

Among the various folks I'm mentoring these days are three Millennials: Kenzie (age 34), Emi (age 27), and Mike (age 29). All are close to the same age as my grandchildren, which allows me to play the grandpa card when needed. Some of you may recognize that card from your experiences with your own grandparents: It typically includes being caring, lovable, and, when the situation calls for it, irascible. Sound familiar?

The coolest thing about mentoring is that both parties have the opportunity to learn from each other—which makes it a mutually beneficial, learning experience. Learning is a good thing, no matter how old we are.

Here are three examples of how I, a bona fide old guy, learned from several of the young folks I mentored. Let's start with Kenzie:

> Kenzie: "Hey, Jim, I'm leaving for Morocco next week. We need to reschedule our next meeting."
>
> Me: "Weren't you just in Hawaii a couple of months ago?"
>
> Kenzie: "Yep."
>
> Me: "Sheesh. How many vacations do you take every year?"
>
> Kenzie: "Jim, maybe you've forgotten, we've talked about this before. My generation doesn't live to work like your generation did. We work to live."

Then there was Emi:

> Me: "I just finished writing my latest book, but I can't figure out how Amazon's publishing platform works. Dealing with that company drives me nuts."
>
> Emi: "So, what's the problem? Just follow the instructions."
>
> Me: "I think they're written in Sewali."
>
> Emi: "I don't read Sewali, Jim, but I'll stop by tomorrow and show you how to do what you need done. Should take ten minutes."

And, finally, Mike:

> Mike: "Hey Jim, have you tried posting some of what you write on Medium yet?"
>
> Me: "What's Medium?"

Mike: "It's a website that publishes blogs and short stories. Last I heard 60 million people a month read their stuff."

Me: "Oh."

Mike: "I thought you were a writer. Every writer should know what Medium is."

Me: "Duh."

Exchanges like these happen all the time, more frequently than you can imagine. In the course of a typical one-hour meeting with people like Kenzie, Emi, or Mike, there's likely to be as many as half a dozen or more eye-opening "aha" moments for me alone. There are times when I wonder which of us is getting more out of our sessions, me or them. I rarely go home disappointed.

The most rewarding and, ultimately, the best learning opportunities come as a mentoring relationship matures. It's hard to imagine a successful mentoring experience that doesn't progress into a friendship. I've been mentoring Kenzie, Emi, and Mike for an average of five years or so now, and have built close, long-lasting friendships with each of them.

This "generation-skipping friendship" is a rewarding unintended consequence of a mentor-mentee relationship. Having a group of friends 50 years younger than me has been energizing and illuminating. And, as you can see by the examples above, educational.

One can only imagine the benefits that can result when a relationship between an octogenarian and a millennial, transitions into a friendship. I gain the perspective of youth while they gain the wisdom of experience.

I'm their ticket to becoming successful.

They're my ticket to staying young.

THE WISDOM:

"You get what you give from a mentoring relationship.

Both parties win."

WHEN YOU WANT TO ZIG AND YOUR SPOUSE WANTS TO ZAG

"A compromise is an agreement whereby both parties get what neither of them wanted."—ANONYMOUS

MY CELL PHONE RANG, BUT NO name popped up on the caller ID. Usually, I let such calls roll over to voice mail; the caller can leave a voice message if she wants me badly enough. Defying the law of averages, I answered this one anyway.

"Hi Jim, this is Shannon," a friendly and familiar voice said. Shannon was a member of a national business group I'd facilitated for twenty years. She and her husband Mike were (and still are) the owners of a successful business in Sacramento. The two were a good match for their family-run business: Shannon managed the operations while Mike oversaw sales. Mrs. Inside and Mr. Outside.

After chatting about her industry and our mutual friends, Shannon said, "Jim, Mike and I are considering acquiring a two-year-old business in Boise, Idaho. Would you help us work through the acquisition process?"

"I'd be happy to," I replied, without hesitation. It sounded like fun. "Would you sell your current business?" I asked.

"No reason to," Shannon said. "We can run it with our eyes closed. Besides, our industry is changing. Tack on the effects of

COVID-19 and it's difficult to grow our business these days. It's pretty much on cruise control."

Over the next few weeks, the three of us Zoomed several times and exchanged a bevy of emails. Shannon and Mike then made a formal offer to purchase the business. When the seller didn't agree with all the terms, Shannon—the designated dealmaker of the two—wouldn't budge. The deal died.

A week or so later I received an email from Shannon. After the acquisition had been killed, she'd asked Mike to backburner his need to pursue any new business opportunities for at least six months. She needed time to relax and catch her breath, she told him; the process they'd just gone through had been time-consuming and stressful.

"Essentially, Jim, the deal fell through when I drew a line in the sand and the seller wasn't amenable to our wishes," she'd said in a subsequent email. Did I think she'd made the right decision to pull the plug on the deal? Was she right to ask Mike to slow down?

I emailed her back. "Shannon, my experience has been that women tend to be more security-conscious than men, especially as age kicks in. Perhaps that's because you know you're going to live longer than us guys, at least two years, the statistics say." With this in mind, I suggested, her line-in-the-sand ultimatum had been, in part, gender driven.

At that point in her life, security trumped risk. I've seen this happen in my house too.

In one of our phone conversations, Shannon had told me she wanted to spend more time with her mom, her aunt, her kids, and her good friends. She'd be content to sit back, chill out, and enjoy the benefits of their years of hard work. Meanwhile Mike, saddled with the ever-simmering DNA of an entrepreneur, will always be on the prowl for his next rodeo. Whether he means to or not.

Shannon's priorities have changed over the years, while Mike's have not. Once an entrepreneur, always an entrepreneur.

Another contributor to their difference in outlook is that Mike will forever be stuck with the two traits that are characteristic of most successful entrepreneurs: a healthy ego and the need to be relevant.

Thanks to many years spent overcoming the risks inherent in owning a business, most successful entrepreneurs develop an ego that can be, on occasion, let's just say, excessive. It comes with the turf for people like him and is difficult to suppress. For better or for worse, Mike is stuck with his ego. And it will never stop needing stoking.

He's also stuck with the need to be relevant. As their company's designated salesperson, the role of always being important to his customers has taken root. Mike still needs to have people look to him for solutions and depend on him to solve their problems. Which is yet another reason why he can't ride off into the sunset like other folks do. He's addicted to being relevant. He needs to be needed.

Years ago, John Gray wrote his seminal book *Men are from Mars, Women are from Venus*. Nowhere is that title more applicable than at this time in Shannon and Mike's life. Shannon needs the time and space to enjoy the relationships that are meaningful to her, while Mike needs a place and opportunity for his adrenalin to run. The two aren't always compatible.

The solution, of course, is compromise. When Mike wants to go south and Shannon's preference is north, east or west may be the best direction.

East or west may not be the perfect direction, but perfection can be elusive. At this point in their life anyway, it's the best direction for their family.

THE WISDOM:

Compromise is not about winning and losing. It's

about caring, then sharing, and finally moving on.

THE TWO BEST WAYS TO
SHARE WISDOM

"I cannot teach anybody anything; I can only make them think."—SOCRATES

RAISE YOUR HAND IF YOU'VE READ the book *Tuesdays with Morrie*. For those of you who didn't raise your hands, I suggest you give it a read. It's a heart warmer as well as a head warmer.

Morrie Schwartz was a philosophy professor at Brandeis University in the 1960s, 1970s, and 1980s. I can picture him now: musty cardigan sweater, hair disheveled, blackboard at the ready. I'm sure he was one of those traditional professors who could talk for hours on whatever topic he chose; he was not only well-versed in philosophy but in just about everything else. The classrooms he taught in back in those days were smaller, friendlier, and cozier, which meant the student/teacher connections were tighter and stronger. When Morrie sneezed, his students ducked.

I'd bet that Morrie knew which of his students were in his class to get a degree and which were there to learn. I'd also bet he knew most by name and that Mitch Albom was one of his favorites. Mitch went on to a career in journalism and then, in 1993, heard that that his old professor was dying of ALS.

Over the next few months, Mitch renewed their friendship and began meeting weekly with Morrie, asking questions and taking notes. Lo and behold, the idea for *Tuesdays with Morrie* was born. The book shares Morrie's wisdom and explores the bond that developed between the two men.

I had a favorite college professor too. His name was Reuben Zubrow and he was challenging, charismatic, and affectionately known as the University of Colorado's larger than life economist. He and I played tennis one time following a class. After he whooped me soundly, we wound down with a couple of beers at The Sink, Boulder's favorite pub. It was there we became good friends. A game of tennis and a couple of beers can do that to people.

Before Professor Zubrow, there was Miss Brodie, my high school English teacher. I wasn't aware of it at the time, but she, along with my mom, were the two people who whetted my appetite for the power of the written word. Mom made sure I was reading the right books while Miss Brodie helped me structure sentences, mind my grammar, and watch out for dangling participles. Unbeknown to Miss Brodie or to me, her teaching would prove to be a powerful motivator in the years following my working career.

Like all of her students, I took Miss Brodie's class and then moved on to the next chapter of life. Following high school, she and I never spoke again. As a result, she never knew the impact she had on my life. Ditto with Professor Zubrow. It would have been the same with Morrie and Mitch I'm sure, had the student not read about his teacher's failing health and taken the initiative to knock on his door.

In some ways, I'd liked to have been a teacher like Morrie or Reuben. Teachers have a wide sphere of influence, providing them with a vast number of opportunities to impact lives. Professor Zubrow had a staggering 43,000 students pass through his classrooms and lecture halls over his 43-year career. That kind of leverage is unimaginable to those of us who have chosen mentoring as our way of teaching. For us, it's one life at a time.

Personally, I've never had the tools or the patience to teach in a classroom. I can't stand still for long periods of time and I don't know enough about anything to be able talk about it for an entire semester. Besides, I'd probably play favorites with the students, favoring those who were there to learn and dissing those who weren't. Professor Zubrow was known to throw erasers at his students who weren't listening. I'd throw pencil sharpeners.

Forty-three thousand students? At best, I can mentor maybe two dozen people at a time. But the good news is that most of my mentoring efforts result in ongoing and long-lasting relationships, so my turnover rate is miniscule. Meanwhile, Morrie and Reuben turned over their classrooms and lecture halls every semester. They touched more lives, but I touched mine more deeply.

It's the depth of a mentoring relationship that makes it so captivating to those of us who do it. We don't just *touch* lives; we envelop them. We know our mentees' families and friends, we hear their dreams and their fears, we share their losses and disappointments. And we watch them grow, in their careers and in their personal lives. In many cases, we know more about what makes our mentees tick than anyone else in their lives, parents, partners, and bosses included.

The brief relationships that come from a classroom don't work for those of us who have chosen mentoring over teaching. Our role is to finish what Morrie, Rueben, and Miss Brodie started.

Not only do we help those we mentor, we also get to see what we've wrought.

THE WISDOM:

Teachers are friendly with their students; mentors

are friends with them.

WITH APOLOGIES TO THE YOUNGER GENERATIONS

"Get involved. You don't want to look back on your life and realize that you successfully managed to stay out of it."—ROBERT BREAULT

DEAR GENXERS, MILLENNIALS, AND GENZERS—

I graduated from college in 1958. President Eisenhower, in his State of the Union address that year, opined about the specter of nuclear war, a looming recession, and economic competition from Japan; that country, the one we were at war with only a dozen or so years ago, was starting to sell cars in the U.S. Which wasn't sitting well with a lot of Americans.

Those were Eisenhower's gravest headaches, as he saw them anyway. I'm willing to bet that you GenXers, Millennials, and GenZer's wish our country's most grievous problems today were that simple. In fact, they're not even close.

Granted, we old people always like to think that things have never been worse than they are in the present. Why, I can remember my mom telling me that she was glad she wasn't growing up in "times like these" when I was in high school. Looking back, my biggest problem was that I wasn't good enough to play on our high school basketball team.

I'm embarrassed to say that the country we're turning over to the Class of '21 makes my Class of '58's world look like we had Camelot served to us on a silver platter.

Here's a smattering of the problems I feel guilty about leaving behind for you young'uns to fix:

The National Debt: Today the U.S. borrows money from its citizens and pays them back tomorrow…with the money they borrow today. Sound familiar? Bernie Madoff went to prison for doing it; so did Charles Ponzi. Our national debt is, at last count, $27 trillion and rising. That's $82,000 for every U.S. citizen, including children.

There's an old saying in the nonprofit world that goes "no money, no mission." That saying also applies to governments; after all, they're nonprofits too. If you believe what that saying states, then the U. S. can't continue this way forever. Right now, we can't pay our bills without borrowing. In my eyes, we're broke.

Climate Change: Many of the climate change issues we're starting to work on should have been addressed 25 years ago. We're late out of the gate, as the horseracing folks like to say. It's impossible to envision what the world's climate is going to look like 50 years from now when you young folks are my age. As I write this, I'm living in Tucson where temperatures can reach 115 degrees in the summers. What will that number be in 2070? Who will be able to live down here then?

Politics, Partisanship, and Polarization: There's no room in the middle for moderates and centrists. I should know, I'm one of them and we've been forgotten, left behind to fend for ourselves. We have a hard time discussing politics and government with people on the right or the left; they get angry if we don't agree with them. People don't just disagree anymore—they take sides.

Income Inequality: There's no middle ground here, either. The top 2% are killing it, while the other 98% are treading water. Or worse. This means our hallowed middle class is shrinking. Sure, business profits are up and, as this is written, the stock market has been on the rise since 2009. But if 98% of Americans are struggling with their financial situation, what matter does a rising stock market make?

Our Reputation: An international organization called the Reputation Institute recently published a study of national reputations. Sweden ranks #1, Canada #6, and the UK #18. The U.S.? We're #36 and fading. We used to be the knights of the world. Now we're the peasants.

The World: The good news is there aren't any world wars going on. Meanwhile, primarily thanks to the coronavirus and weak leadership from just about every nation including ours, the world is in disarray and there's no one around to help clean up the mess. That includes the U.S.; we're too busy trying to cure what ails us to help anyone else.

Anyway, for what it's worth, I apologize to you younger generations for all the sinister stuff that's going on today. I wish I were speaking on behalf of *all* of the Boomer and Silent Generation members, but I haven't been so anointed. So I'm apologizing on behalf of myself.

There's one piece of good news, however. We're Americans. When something's busted, we've always fixed it. When something's gone wrong, we've always made it go right. And when someone's needed our help, we've always come to their aid.

Yes, we're Americans and making things right is what we've been bred to do.

We've survived a shit storm of problems over the life of our country: One Civil War, two World Wars, and the Great Depression, not to mention the Viet Nam War, 9/11, and now COVID-19, which is a long way from being over.

My mom used to say that where there's a problem, there's an opportunity. If she was right, then you have a world of opportunities awaiting you.

All you have to do is step up.

With hope,
Jim Schell

THE WISDOM:

If the U.S. can survive the Civil War we can

survive where we are today. Will the next

Abraham Lincoln please stand up.

PART THREE

The Wisdom We Learn from the World Around Us

The world is changing, and it's changing fast. You'd better get on board or you'll miss the train.

HOW TO LEARN EVERYTHING YOU NEED TO KNOW ABOUT SOMEONE IN ONLY FOUR HOURS

"They say golf is like life, but don't believe them.
Golf is more complicated than that."
—GARDNER DICKINSON

LET'S SAY YOU'RE A KID AND you want to grow up and become a doctor—or maybe a teacher or a coach or a leader of people. To pursue any of those vocations, you'll first need to understand what it is that makes people tick: how they think, feel, and act.

Given that need for understanding, where would you go to gather the knowledge?

Well, you could go to college, of course. Once there, you'd read books and listen to lectures, and spend four years learning everything you need to know about how people think, feel, and act. You'd probably also shell out big bucks for the privilege.

Then, once you've finished your college career, you'd be ready to face the world with a firm understanding of the infinite mystery of us homo sapiens—one step closer to becoming the doctor, teacher, trainer, or leader of people that you set out to be. After all, you now know the deep-seated secrets that determine how all of us think, feel, and act.

But, wait, what if there was another option? One that wouldn't consume four years of your life and wouldn't cost you or your parents boatloads of hard-earned money? Oh, and lest I forget, you'd have fun doing it.

Ready for the answer?

Call your local golf course. Get a tee time.

Yep, you heard it here first. Play golf.

I've been playing golf for 76 years now and I know, yes I KNOW, that you can learn everything you need to know about how people think, feel, and act by playing a round of golf with them. That's all you need, just one measly round.

OK, so I'll admit that this golf-life metaphor may be a bit of a stretch. Chances are you wouldn't be qualified to be a doctor, teacher, coach, or a leader of people after playing four years of golf instead of attending four or more years of college. But you would be able to determine who, among the people you've played golf with, you'd most like to have as your friend or confidant or teammate or soul mate or partner. One piddly round of golf—four hours in the invigorating out-of-doors—is all that it takes.

Intrigued? Here's how it works. Let's say the person you're playing that round of golf with...

> ...is ten minutes late showing up. (You've just learned she thinks her time is more valuable than yours.)
>
> ...misses a short putt and spits out a juicy phrase that even George Carlin wouldn't understand. (You've just learned he has a temper problem—and probably a decorum one, too.)
>
> ...after looking to see if you're watching, she nudges her ball ever so slightly in order to improve her lie, which is against the gentlemanly rules of golf. (You've just learned not to give her your password. Or anything else of value.)
>
> ...coughs in the middle of your backswing. (You've just learned he either has the sniffles or wants to win no matter what it takes.)
>
> ...wolfs down three drinks following the game while you're still adding up the score. (You've just learned that booze is her friend.)

...doesn't offer to pay for either the golf or the drinks. (You've just learned his social skills suck. And he's a tight-wad to boot.)

I've been playing this frustrating, time-consuming, character-re-vealing, head-gnashing game of golf for 76 years. I can't remember the number of strokes I took in yesterday's game, but I sure *can* remember the people I was playing with when I took those strokes. And I can remember their character, too. Or lack thereof.

Golf keeps no secrets about those of us who play it.

We are how we play the game.

THE WISDOM:

People are open books, and a golf course is the easiest,

quickest and most enjoyable place to read them.

STOP COMPLAINING ABOUT THE GOVERNMENT, DO THIS INSTEAD

"It's always better to light the candle than curse the darkness."—NANCY JACOBSON

IF I WAS A TEACHER AND my students were our federal and state governments, here are two of the grades I'd hand out:

My Former Home State of Oregon	D
The U.S. Government	F–

Furthermore, if there was a grade lower than F–, that's what the Feds would get. And if I was a resident of California or Illinois, I'd boot those governments out of school. They wouldn't get a grade.

I'm not a teacher. Rather, I'm a former small business owner/ entrepreneur. Since the years following the sale of my fourth and final business (1990), I've learned that I enjoy fixing broken organizations, both for-profits and nonprofits. As a result, I look at the U.S. and Oregon governments through that fix-it lens and wonder what I could do to straighten them out.

The answer: Not much.

They're too big for little guys like me. Too cumbersome. Too cavernous. And, sad to say, too screwed up. Which makes them out of my comfort zone, not to mention my skill set. There are times when I wonder, given the degree of our governments' declining performances since the turn of this century, whether or not they can ever be fixed.

Further pondering of our nation's governmental messes makes me wonder whether we average citizens should be spending our time grousing about our various government's miserable state of affairs. Should we be firing off letters to the editor complaining about the way things are? Should we be lighting up our Facebook page with angry rants? Should we be hanging out on downtown street corners waving signs and hollering at passing motorists?

What good does all that do, other than making the person doing the hollering feel better? Since when will shouting from the street corner change a motorist's mind? Would all that hollering and shouting and waving of signs really be the best use of our time?

As someone who's tried and/or observed several all of those tactics, I've learned one thing for sure. I've learned that employing those tactics is not the best use of my time. Besides, I'm not loud or obnoxious enough, and my patience has a short fuse. I'd have trouble shrugging off the cursers and bird flippers.

I'm not saying that dissent, organized or otherwise, is a bad thing; we all have a constitutional right to have our opinions heard. As Martin Luther King Jr. decisively proved, a collection of united voices can make a difference. But dissent without action is not a viable long-term solution for what ails us. Certainly, I'm interested in your opinion, but what I'm more interested in is what you're going to do about whatever it is you believe.

In other words, what actions have you taken to resolve the problems you're so pissed off about?

Before you throw up your hands in desperation about the plight of our governments, I have a not-very-unique-but-potentially-meaningful suggestion for you to consider. Rather than spending your time complaining about the things you can't impact, why don't you start working on those things you can? Why don't you try making a difference at home, in your own backyard, where your presence can be felt? Where you can be a big fish in a small pond, instead of a small fish in a big pond?

Most of us ordinary citizens can't make a difference in DC or our state's capitals, but we sure can right at home. For instance, we can...

> **Help a nonprofit:** There are somewhere around 100 impactful social service nonprofits in my hometown of Bend, population 100,000. Imagine how many must there be in NYC or LA! They all need boards of directors, volunteers, and donors.
>
> **Help a local government:** Most local governments (city and county) have a long list of committees that are seeking citizens to provide them with perspective and advice on how to make their community or region a better place to live. Call the government in question or inquire at your local Chamber of Commerce.
>
> **Help a neighborhood:** Many neighborhoods have associations designed to make their neck of the woods a better place to raise kids or grow old. If your neighborhood doesn't have one, get busy. Start one.
>
> **Start a business:** A recent poll sponsored by the Kaufman Foundation discovered that today's Baby Boomers are significantly more likely to start a business than are today's Millennial. So, if you're a boomer, and golf isn't enough, check with your local SBDC (Small Business Development Center) and learn how to start a business.

And that's not all you can do. You can also shop at local businesses (thereby creating local jobs). You can donate to local causes. You can volunteer for community events. You can recycle.

And, of course, now more than ever...YOU CAN VOTE!

THE WISDOM:

Get involved. It'll be good for your soul and better

for your community.

THE RISE OF THE BIG GUYS

"I run on coffee, wine, and Amazon Prime"—UNKNOWN

WHEN I WAS A KID, I can still remember going grocery shopping with my mom at Matulef's neighborhood grocery store, corner of Chamberlain and 42nd St. in Des Moines. Matulef's was the largest store in a mishmash of mom-and-pop shops on that corner, which also included Reed's ice cream shop at the far end of the street. That random collection of small businesses would be the predecessor of today's strip mall.

As part of the sacrifice of World War II, Mom and I would stand in line at Matulef's and wait for our family's weekly allotment of bread. Mr. Matulef himself would do the doling out; he knew most of the people in line by their first name. With him doing the apportioning, everyone was sure to get their fair share.

"Good morning, Mrs. Schell," he'd greet Mom, before tousling my hair and holding out a meaty hand for me to shake.

"Do you have any fresh pork chops today?" Mom would ask. "The ones we bought two weeks ago were wonderful."

"There'll be a new order in tomorrow," Matulef would reply. "But we do have a fresh delivery of ground beef right now. If you want some you should get it this morning. It'll be gone by afternoon."

And so turned the wheels of commerce in my neighborhood back in those days. You knew the store owner and he knew you. He knew what you wanted (or what he thought you wanted), and you hoped he had what you were looking for. If he didn't, you'd begrudgingly go somewhere else to find it. Most of the time his inventory-management system, which was largely confined to his head, worked like a well-oiled machine.

Today, Matulef's grocery is no more. Sometime after I graduated from high school and left Des Moines, Matulef's moved on and a Dahl's Grocery took over the space. Then, by the next time I visited Des Moines, Dahl's was history, too. Today there's no grocery store at all in the neighborhood; you have to drive a goodly number of miles to find one of the chains. It's a shame Mr. Matulef isn't around anymore, we could have used his doling-out expertise when we faced the Great Toilet Paper Shortage scare in March of 2020.

This transition away from owner-operated stores like Matulef's began with the advent of Walmart in 1962 and has been gaining steam ever since. When Walmart moves in, small businesses move out. Sure, you get lower prices and wider choices from Walmart, but price and choice can't take the place of Mr. Matulef when rationing time comes around. Besides, who at Walmart can tell you when a fresh batch of pork chops will be on the shelves?

Do I shop at Walmart? Yes (blush), I do. Sporadically. And reluctantly.

Would I shop at Matulef's if it were still around? You betcha, if it had even close to what I needed. And therein lies the rub. In too many cases, Matulef's probably wouldn't have what I needed.

Mary's an egg lover and, a year ago, we needed an egg cooker in our house. Walmart had a half dozen choices on their shelf; Target probably did, too. I bought ours from Walmart.

Would I have a problem with Matulef's higher prices on food and goods? I wouldn't, especially since Matulef's would be sponsoring a Little League team and Mr. Matulef himself would be a member of our local Rotary Club. Additionally, any profits he made would be re-circulated in Des Moines.

OK, so I'll admit it, I'm probably not your average American shopper. Price is the number one draw for a lot of folks while service is secondary. Which is why Walmart is thriving and Matulef's is no longer around. The transition was inevitable, I guess, if it hadn't been Walmart, it would have been another chain.

Interestingly enough, in a fascinating what-goes-around-comes-around scenario, today Amazon is doing to Walmart what Walmart did to Matulef's. Egg cookers? Amazon had a dozen choices I later discovered, ranging from $14.99 to $39.95. Meanwhile, Walmart had a picked-over selection of a half-dozen or so. The prices were similar.

Back in the 1970s and on through 2010 or so, the shopping choices were David vs. Goliath. Today it's Goliath vs. Goliath. The world's largest retailer (Walmart) vs. the world's second largest (Amazon). And Number Two is growing a heck of a lot faster than Number One, which means that it's only a matter of time until the two change places. The predator is being preyed upon.

Today, Walmart is, uncharacteristically, the underdog. The underlying issue here is bricks and mortar vs. technology. Personally, I'd put my money on tech.

If you're wondering what Wall Street thinks about those two companies, here's an interesting tidbit. Amazon, at $1.7 trillion (trillion!), is valued at four times what poor little Walmart is.

But Amazon needs to tread carefully, the goliaths are getting too big, or so our government perceives anyway. The trust busters will be taking a long, hard look at them in the upcoming years. Plus, there's a negative perception these days of tech businesses in general and the Big Four (Facebook, Alphabet/Google, Apple, and Amazon) in particular. The public perception is that they love their technology more than they love their customers.

If Matulef's were still in business today, it'd be the other way around.

THE WISDOM:

Bigger isn't always better, but bigger usually wins.

WHAT TO DO WHEN THE HELP DESK DOESN'T HELP

"It takes months to find a customer and seconds to lose one."—VINCE LOMBARDI

HOW MANY TIMES HAS THE FOLLOWING happened to you? You call a large business's customer service line. You explain your problem to someone who's paid to talk with disgruntled customers. Or at least you try and explain the problem, but the person you're talking to either can't understand your problem or is unable to resolve it.

Frustrated, you finally ask the voice on the other end of the phone, "Who *can* solve my problem?"

"I'm sorry sir," the voice says, unfazed. "I'll transfer you to my supervisor." Thirty minutes and a lot of bad music later, you hang up. You don't care how much their stock sells for on the New York Stock Exchange, you're not a fan.

Time wasted: 45 minutes.
Typical result: No solution. And you're pissed.

This is exactly what happened to Mary a couple of days ago. The problem started when the company in question—Waste Management, in case you're wondering—billed us $50 for being late on a payment, when, in fact, the account was set up for automatic deduction. How can that happen?

The following morning, instead of calling customer service and wasting another 45 minutes of her time, Mary developed her own complaint management procedure. She called the company's billing department instead of customer service. Her call went through without a wait.

"I'd like to pay my bill in full and cancel my service," she said tersely.

"I can do that for you," came a woman's soft-spoken reply. "But would you mind taking a few minutes to explain why."

Mary took a few minutes and explained why.

"What if I were to refund your $50, give you a $25 credit, and make sure that what happened to you won't happen again," the voice cooed. "Would you continue to let us collect your garbage?"

"Well, yes, I suppose," Mary replied, reluctantly. It'd be a whole lot easier than setting up a new account with a competitor.

Time spent: Ten minutes.
Result: A semi-happy Mary.

I have nothing against Waste Management, or any other company that attempts to keep its costs under control. I'd try to keep them under control too, if I were them. But the money they save by hiring folks who aren't trained or equipped or capable to solve customers' problems is wasted when a steamed-up customer makes a beeline for the exit. You'd think they'd learn.

I wonder if Waste Management or any of its goliath peers have figured out that if they do the job properly at the front end, they wouldn't have to spend so much time and money on the backend. Sure sounds like a logical decision to me.

I'd bet dollars to donuts that if Amazon were to start thinking about getting into the garbage-hauling business, Waste Management would make some changes in the quality of its customer service. The specter of Amazon stalking your customers will do that to you.

Until Amazon decides to get in the garbage business, however, it will have to be us, the customer, who does the changing. When there's a problem, we should pick up the phone and call the company's billing department, or Human Resources, or the CEO's assistant, in lieu of customer service.

Mary stopped by my office to gloat after the phone call. "That's it for calling customer service," she said. "From now on I'm calling the finance department first."

"You know, Jim, I just don't get it," she said, her brow furrowed. "We do one transaction a month with Waste Management and yet I have to call their customer service department. Meanwhile, we do half-a-dozen transactions a month with Amazon and they don't even *have* a customer service department, to the best of my knowledge anyway. Or, if they do, I've never talked to them. Maybe they should get in the garbage business."

Yikes! We've been married too long.

THE WISDOM:

A problem is an opportunity in disguise.

Don't screw the problem up twice.

WHY I DON'T LIKE FACEBOOK BUT KEEP SCROLLING ANYWAY

"Thank God for Facebook. Otherwise, I'd have to call 674 people and tell them I just went to the gym." —UNKNOWN

WHEN MY GRANDKIDS WERE YOUNGER, THEY spent more time on Facebook than they did on their homework, dinner, and chores. Combined. I should know, I was a Facebook Grandpa back in those days, keeping track of who their friends were, how their sports teams fared, and what they were doing with their lives.

These days, Facebook is way too uncool for my grandkids and their Millennial friends. After all, they're only a text away from keeping up with the people they care about. They also have Instagram and SnapChat and WhatsApp and God-Knows-What-App at their fingertips. Besides, they don't want to be hanging out at the same places where their parents or grandparents are. How uncool would that be?

Unlike us old folks, our grandkids have better things to do with their time then watch cat and dog videos. So, RIP Facebook. Well, for the Millennials anyway, and presumably for the GenZs right behind them.

Facebook isn't dead for me, however. I'm *not* a text away from my friends because a lot of them don't text. Or if they do, they text me back a month after I've texted them. These days I use Facebook to keep up with selected friends, or at least those that Facebook, in their infinite wisdom, decides to include in my News Feed. Most importantly, however, I use Facebook to keep up with all those cute and funny cat and dog videos.

Personally, I'm a dog guy and not a cat guy but, man, those cats can be funny. Goats are a stitch, too.

(Don't judge. When you get to be 84, you'll watch dog and cat videos, too. You'll see).

With my grandkids doing whatever it is they do on their other digital platforms, I'm no longer a Facebook Grandpa. Rather, I'm a Facebook Lurker. I'm also an armchair psychologist, with people who post on Facebook as my unwitting patients. I read their posts and try to figure out why they said what they said so that I can type-cast them. There's a proud parent here, a lonely ex-spouse there, and, whoops, there's the Russian government trying to rile me up about something.

Yes sir, there's something for everyone on Facebook, but not all of those somethings have my best interests in mind.

Me? I rarely post. I don't want any Facebook Lurkers typecasting me.

Call me corny, but I still enjoy scrolling down my newsfeed and looking for my peeps. (See how I can be hip using Facebook lingo?) If I weren't spending my time on Facebook, I'd be doing something else that would be an even bigger waste of time—like watching TV.

But here's what I don't understand. Facebook is a tech company, right? And people who work for tech companies are younger and supposedly smarter than the rest of us. I know this because, as I mentioned in the Introduction, Mark Zuckerberg said so. So today Facebook has 45,000 smart employees and a founder who dropped out of Harvard (because presumably he wasn't learning enough) and who is, at this moment in time, the fifth richest person in the world.

And yet, Facebook, with all its cool technology and all its smart employees, has screwed up so many things over the years. Their biggest screw up? The lack of advance thought they gave to what the world's bad guys would do with their platform. For every mom, dad, and grandparent that uses Facebook, there's a weirdo, pervert, or foreign government lurking in the background, intent on messing with the minds and lives of us everyday folks. In other words, for every good person on FB, there's a bad one too.

Wouldn't you think that Facebook would have given some thought on how to deal with those assbites early on? Wouldn't you think they'd have built safeguards into their systems to make the perverts go away? I mean, they can tell us what brand of shampoo works best for our hair, but they can't keep the schmucks off our newsfeed. How can that be?

Technology has wrought so many changes in the way we live. Apple, Google, Amazon, Microsoft, and a host of other tech companies have made their mark on our lives. The world is, on balance, a better place to live with those companies doing the stuff they do.

Sorry, but I can't say the same for Facebook.

THE WISDOM:

Sugar, alcohol, and Facebook have one thing in common. None of them are good for us, and yet we indulge in them anyway.

TALLYING YOUR MISTAKES

"I never lose. I either win or learn."
——NELSON MANDELA

EVERY SUCCESSFUL EMPLOYEE, EMPLOYER, PARENT, OR student has learned that it's okay to screw up now and then—as long as we don't screw up in the same way twice.

While mistakes play a major role in both our work and our personal lives, some of us make more of them than others. I was a mistake-making pacesetter in my early small business days, especially in those pre-*Inc.* magazine years when trial-and-error was the number one learning tool for people like me. I'd set out to implement the latest business fad or idea and then, when it failed—as it often did—I'd go back to square one and start all over again.

The good news about trial-and-error as a learning tool is that the lessons we learn from it will remain with us forever. Brains are strange: They sometimes forget the things we do right but they always retain those we mess up.

The bad news? The lessons we learn from messing things up are so godawful expensive. Which is probably the reason why our brains don't forget them. Mess with our pocketbook and we remember.

But mistakes are part of living: As we stumble along life's rocky pathway our mistakes will continue to add up. And up. And so will the price we pay to make them.

———

Several years ago, at the suggestion of a friend, I decided to compile a list of my biggest, most painful mistakes. I accomplished this by writing what is known in some circles as a "Failure Resume." A Failure Resume is the polar opposite of the ubiquitous Professional Resume, which is a compilation of our proudest (and oft-inflated) successes, while a Failure Resume is a compilation of our biggest and most expensive mistakes.

I decided to compile mine to remind myself of the price I'd paid at the time I screwed whatever it was up. More importantly however, I did it to see what I'd learned from those screwups.

Compiling a Failure Resume is no easy task, especially if you're one of those folks who are unwilling to acknowledge your mistakes. Fortunately, that's one problem I don't have (probably because I've made so many of them), so onward I plunged into the unpleasant task. Then, upon completion, I shared my Failure Resume with a friend who had assembled one of his own. We compared our life's biggest screw ups over a beer, a humbling experience and one I wouldn't recommend for those with thin skin.

I won't bore you, or embarrass myself, by sharing all of my greatest screw ups with you, but here's one example:

Mistake: My freshman year at the University of Colorado I "earned" a GPA of 1.56. 2.0 is passing. Excessive partying was the symptom; immaturity was the cause.
Result: My mom and dad exiled me to Drake University in Des Moines where I spent my sophomore year. Living at home. With my parents. Ouch.
Lesson learned: When you shirk your responsibilities, you pay the price.

Remember my story in Part One ("How I Found a Career I Could Love") about my failed ice arena? Now there was a juicy mistake and yet it led to a major change in my life. From it I learned that I needed to be my own boss. That lesson would eventually lead to a successful and rewarding career.

There is, of course, one surefire way to avoid mistakes. Stock up on Cheetos and beer, hunker down on your Barcalounger, and turn on the TV.

Sure enough, you won't be making any mistakes.

THE WISDOM:

We can't learn from our mistakes unless we first

acknowledge that we made them.

WHEN THE FIREFLIES ARE GONE

"What's the use of a fine house if you haven't got a tolerable planet to put it on?"
—HENRY DAVID THOREAU

SEVERAL MONTHS AGO, GLOBAL WARMING SUDDENLY became personal to me. Oh, I've been a believer in it for a couple of decades now, but its symptoms have either been so far away or its implications so vast that I couldn't identify with the problem. Vast, as in its impact on oceans, rainforests, glaciers, ice floes, and the ozone level, for instance, right on down to the plight of the Monarch butterfly. (Can you imagine a world without *them?*)

I've read about most of global warming's symptoms but until recently I haven't felt, touched, or personally experienced any that have knocked my socks off. Until, that is, I stumbled across an article about the plight of the lowly firefly. The gist of the article was that the innocent, mind-its-own-business firefly is disappearing from the face of our earth. As in going away. Forever.

I don't know how important fireflies are globally, but I do know how important they were to my childhood. I'm sure they had an impact on a lot of other folks who remember the dancing, blinking bugs. I know there are lots of those folks because there's an international nonprofit that follows what is happening to the firefly. You can check it out at firefly.org. Once there you'll be gobsmacked by the organization's rallying call: GLOWING, GLOWING, GONE.

If you're a firefly fan and that tagline doesn't grab you, nothing will.

I'll admit that fireflies may not be worth a second thought to people who haven't experienced them, but they bring back fond memories to me, just as polar bears, whales, and pandas might do to other folks around the world. If you grew up in downtown LA or Singapore, you wouldn't know a firefly from a barn cat. Given that lack of association, I can understand why most people wouldn't be overly concerned if the firefly's lights were to go out.

On the other hand, if you grew up in Iowa (or just about any place east of Kansas), lightening bugs—our name for fireflies—can be found in the same memory bucket as hopscotch, Annie-Annie-Over, and Elvis Presley.

When I was a kid and the summer nights were warm, my sister Chris and I would ask Mom for a mason jar. We'd punch holes in the tin lid, then throw some grass and an apple slice in the jar; the grass provides a place for the lightening bugs to hide, the apple slice gives them something to hold onto. Then we'd chase their pulsating lights around our backyard, filling that mason jar with dozens of blinking bugs. If you haven't been treated to the spectacle of a gaggle of giggling kids with mason jars in their hands chasing blinking lights in a neighborhood backyard in the dark, you've missed a picture that would make a Norman Rockwell painting.

The following morning we'd set our pulsating captives free, like fly fisherman do when returning trout to their native streams. Every trout counts, the theory goes, and so does every lightening bug.

This news about the, uh, dim future of lightening bugs is heartbreaking. Here I am, 75 years past my lightening bug days, suddenly being told that they could be gone forever, with global warming the culprit. It's one thing if Polar Bears are a threatened species, but, c'mon man, no more lightening bugs?

Now don't get me wrong. I'm also a big fan of almost all of God's creatures (mosquitoes and rattlesnakes excepted) and the loss of most of them would be devastating. I'm only making the point that we'd miss the most that which we've personally experienced.

Global warming impacts us all in so many ways: extreme weather, shrinking polar regions, rising oceans, air pollution, population displacement…the list goes on. One man's lightning bug is another man's polar bear. We're all in this together.

Recently, in a conversation with a fellow octogenarian, we agreed that we're relieved we won't be around twenty-five years from now. The world will be way too different then—and not all in a good way. I'm sure our parents said the same thing when we were growing up, but this time it's different. (Isn't it always?) My aging friend and I believe the world *is* going to be hugely different because global warming is so far-reaching. So universal. And so pervasive.

How did things go so wrong so fast, we wondered? The modern form of humans has been around for 200,000 years or more. Why did the world wait so long to get dumped on by global warming— or at least to recognize that it's a problem? While global warming activism began in the early 1990's, the topic didn't become top of mind until the early aughts. And it wasn't until just recently it came to the attention of today's world leaders who are in a position to do something about it.

I know my generation is partly to blame for where we are today. Even more complicit are my generation's successors, our Baby Boomer offspring who have been in the positions of power for the last twenty years. We all should have known better. And we all should have started to do something about it. Sooner rather than later.

Can we really expect to make the climate less extreme again? Can we really expect to make the rainforests healthy and replace the Amazon's felled trees? Can we really expect to make the Artic habitable for the disappearing polar bears?

We'll never know unless we try.

THE WISDOM:

Global warming: It isn't like we haven't seen it coming.

BOOKS: WE'D BE NONE THE WISER WITHOUT THEM

"Those who don't read have no advantage over those who can't read."—ANONYMOUS

KNOWING MY MOM, WE PROBABLY HAD the following discussion sometime around 1948 when she would have seen me doing something that she deemed to be a waste of time. This would happen just about every day, especially during the dog days of summer.

Mom would have started off the conversation with a comment that went something like this...

"Jim, have you read all the Hardy Boys books we gave you for Christmas?" Some kids got baseball gloves or bikes. I got books.

"Mom, I finished the last one a month ago."

"Hmmm," she would have muttered while straightening the bun on the back of her head. "Can you think of anything unusual or unique that you might be interested in reading about and learning? Something you won't be reading in school?"

"Well, I saw a Buck Rogers comic book yesterday. He does a lot of neat stuff in outer space."

"You mean you might be interested in learning about astronomy?"

"Well, yeah. Astronomy."

Then Mom and I went to the library, which in turn led me to check out a book on astronomy, which in turn led to a throbbing headache. A dozen or so pages into the book, I quickly realized that math and physics were key elements in the study of astronomy. Yet math and physics were the precursor to headaches, for me anyway. Buck Rogers must have been an incredibly smart dude to do all the rocket ship, outer space, planet hopping kind of stuff he did, but you wouldn't know it from his comic books. He seemed like just another Superman to me.

What really happened there was that at age 12, for the first time in my life, I actually set out to research a subject that would have positively impacted my life. Astronomy ended up not being my thing, but that trip to the library was my first experience at voluntarily looking for a nonfiction book that could have led me to a meaningful hobby or useful knowledge.

Experiences such as this came about because my mom was a book lover and never went a day without reading one. She was a longtime member of the Book of the Month Club and would devour the latest *Reader's Digest* the same day it came in the mail. Thanks to her, I'd turned into a reader myself by the time I was a teen—another gift for which I can't thank her enough.

As a kid, I read mostly fiction, especially Jack London and Ernest Hemingway, two authors who wrote about the kind of stuff my friends and I liked to daydream about. As an adult, I switched to nonfiction; if a book was about business or self-improvement, I'd gobble it up like a Thanksgiving turkey. Ken Blanchard, Tom Peters, Jim Collins, and Stephen Covey were a few of my favorites.In later years, the bookshelves in my home office overflowed with dusty, frayed, and marked up books, driving Mary, the queen of order, neatness, and cleanliness, crazy.

My infatuation with nonfiction continued when, after selling my final business in 1990, I decided I wanted to be on the active, rather than the passive, end of books. I wanted to be an author. A published author.

Fast forward to today. Writing has overtaken playing golf and petting our dogs as my favorite thing to do. One of the coolest things about writing is that it can actually get better with age, which is counter to just about everything else that is happening to people my age these days.

Warren Buffet, a guy who's been around the block even more times than I have, says he speed reads 500 pages a day. That's two books a day or 730 books a year. I'm sure he can afford them.

Bill Gates is another raving fan of reading, albeit one who's easier to emulate than Buffet. Gates reads a book a week and never starts one without finishing it, no matter how crummy the book turns out to be. Gates is one of those readers who fills a book's margins with his thoughts and takeaways. I wonder if he does that so no one will want to borrow them.

Buffet and Gates also have one more similarity where reading is concerned: They don't read to be entertained; they read to be educated. Which means most of what they read is nonfiction.

I mentioned earlier that Mary and I sold our Bend house and relocated to Tucson. At the time we sold it, we were in a serious downsizing mode, so I made the painful decision that I no longer needed 90% of the books in my office. After all, I no longer needed to know how to make a PowerPoint presentation, how to use LinkedIn, or how to build a website. Sorting through those dusty piles of books was a reminder of the twists and turns of my life. Books and nostalgia are never far apart.

It's one thing to downsize by moving into a smaller home or buying a car that gets better gas mileage. But cleaning out a lifetime collection of books?

That turned out to be the toughest downsize of them all.

THE WISDOM:

Books: Where else can one learn a life-changing

lesson and then follow it up with a nap?

SHIFTING GEARS: WHEN READER TURNS WRITER

"Get it down. Take chances. It may be bad but it's the only way you can write anything good."
—WILLIAM FAULKNER

THE PACKAGE IS ON THE WAY, I was told. It should be here by this Wednesday, they said. If UPS did what they're being paid to do, they added.

I took them on their word, which meant that on Wednesday I stayed home all day, waiting for the UPS truck to deliver The Package. Except that UPS didn't show, so at the end of the day, there I still stood, Package-less.

Since UPS is a reputable company, I was sure that The Package would be delivered on Thursday. So I cancelled my golf game and once again stayed home all day. Wouldn't you know it; the people in brown failed me again. Still no Package.

At 6am on Friday I phoned the east coast company that reportedly sent The Package to me. Once again, I was assured it had gone out as previously stated. They did their best, they said. It was UPS's fault.

The year was 1991, incidentally, which meant that today's sophisticated tracking services weren't available. I had no choice. I waited.

And so it was that on a sunny Friday in San Diego, I stayed home yet again. Finally, at 2:36pm, the knock on the front door came. I threw open the door and there stood a man in brown, clutching a package. The Package. My package.

"It's here," I gurgled, struggling to retain my composure. I signed the receipt and snatched The Package from the man's hand. I closed the door, shouted for Mary, and grabbed the knife I'd placed on the hallway table in preparation for this moment.

In less time than it would take for me to say "my dream come true," I opened the box. Mary was standing beside me as I reached inside and pulled out the object of my frenzy. It felt exactly as I thought it would: slick, bold, and fresh, looking grand in its shiny new jacket. I held it up for Mary to see.

There it gleamed, *The Brass Tacks Entrepreneur* by Jim Schell. MY FIRST-EVER PUBLISHED BOOK!

Which meant I was, as of that moment, a published author.

A tad over-dramatic perhaps? Well, maybe, but remember, those were the days before self-publishing. Having a book published by a real live New York Publisher (Henry Holt) *was* a big deal. To give you an idea why I was so giddy, here's a collection of unofficial statistics that I remember gathering during those mid-1990s days of book publishing:

- 2 million people a year start to write a book
- 750,000 finish it
- 50,000 get it published
- 5,000 make appreciable money from it

I was one of that 50,000! A year or so later that book would quietly go out of print, which meant I would not be one of the hallowed 5,000. I'd been given a $10,000 advance and the book had sold enough copies so I wouldn't have to repay any of it. Within the following two years, my next two books followed a similar path. Stephen King, I'm sure, breathed a sigh of relief.

The reality is that if you're an author not named Stephen King and you sell $10,000 worth of books over a lifetime, you're doing just fine compared to the industry as a whole. Whether you like it or not, it also means that your writing is a hobby, not a career. Or a business.

My fourth published book crossed the line. I co-authored *Small Business for Dummies* in 1998 and today, 22 years and five editions later, that book is still going strong. It's sold well over 750,000 copies and is marching happily onward, thanks to the iconic Dummies brand. Without that brand, that book would have ended up in the publisher's remainder pile, similar to my earlier ones.

For those who hanker to make a living as a writer, the odds against you becoming a Grisham, Covey, or Chopra are daunting, verging on impossible. You won't even be a Schell unless you can come up with a Dummies title that has yet to be written. Or unless you're a marketing genius or can write a killer book *and* find a killer agent.

Today, thanks to self-publishing, it's easy to publish a book, whether it's good, bad, or ugly. Amazon doesn't care who you are or what your subject matter is; they'll publish it anyway. They'll also provide a venue for you to sell it and will collect the proceeds and deposit them in your bank account. All you have to do is write the damn thing.

Oh yes, lest I forget, you'll also need to figure out how to motivate readers to purchase the book. Amazon doesn't do that, or at least they don't do it for free. The selling and marketing of your book will, I assure you, be one hell of a lot harder than writing the damn thing.

My intent here is not to discourage you from writing the book of your dreams, but rather to help you understand the reality of making appreciable money from it. Heck, if you want to write a book for the sake of being able to say you're a published author, then get cracking. Go ahead. Write it.

It won't pay your bills, but it will feed your ego, which is almost as good.

THE WISDOM:

Writing a book is a labor of love. Selling a book is a labor of marketing. The two are usually done by different people.

THE BEST QUESTION YOU CAN EVER ASK

"Judge a man by his questions rather than his answers."—VOLTAIRE

I LOVE QUESTIONS. I ESPECIALLY LOVE asking them and then watching people scratch their heads as they try to come up with an answer. One of the reasons I'm so stoked about questions is that I've had plenty of practice asking them, which means I can ask zinger ones. I'm not so hot at answering them however, especially when dates, times, places, and names are involved. Don't invite me to your trivia party.

Never underestimate the role that questions play in your life. Think about it. Every decision you make during the day—and you make dozens (hundreds?) of them—is preceded by a subconscious question. What time should you get out of bed in the morning? What should you have for lunch? Should you wear a mask before going out? How do you get your kid to stop playing computer games? Who should you vote for? What should you read before bedtime? On and on the questions emerge, like cookies out of Mrs. Field's oven.

While we all have a long list of mundane questions that we ask ourselves daily, there are also life-altering and deal-breaking questions that shape our lives and impact our future. Is this the person you want to spend the rest of your life with? Is this the right career for you? Which school should you encourage your kid to attend? Now that you're 50, should you buy a BMW or stick with a Jeep? Has the time finally come to get hearing aids? You name the question and most of us older folks have asked it at one time or another.

Questions can come from everywhere, from anyone, at any time of our life. "What's up doc?" Bugs Bunny used to ask when we were kids. "Where's the beef?" Wendy's wanted to know as we got older. "What's your greatest accomplishment?" our grandkids ask us today. "Is there an afterlife?" some of us wonder as we get older.

Then there are the light and playful questions we like to ask because we want to put someone on the spot or because we want to kick off a lively discussion. These are the questions that can make us laugh, cringe, or scratch our head.

Here's one of my favorite discussion-baiting questions. I ask this question often; it's an ideal way to begin a mentoring session: "What's the number one exciting thing going on in your life right now?"

Then you get to watch the askee's face light up as she tells you the coolest, most interesting thing that's going on in her life. Whammo, the session's off to a luscious beginning.

Or there's the polar opposite of that "exciting thing" question: "What's the number one problem that's keeping you up at night?"

This question is yet another discussion-baiting way to kick off a mentoring session or break the ice when sharing a beer with a friend.

My all-time favorite question is one that I'm liable to foist on folks at any time and in any place. Friends, mentees, students, waitresses, sons, daughters, neighbors…no one is safe from this question when I'm around. My favorite target is someone with a spark in her eye and a jaunty look on her face—the look of a person who's likely to respond to an engaging question with an interesting answer:

"If this was a perfect world," I begin, "what will you be doing five years from now?"

If the time is right and I'm right about the askee, that question will either produce a frown or a smile, to be followed by the revelation of a festering dream or a percolating vision. Which will, in turn, set off a whole new series of questions, and when we're finished, the askee will have floored me with all kinds of revealing answers. If the time is absolutely, positively right, she just might floor herself with her answer too. Such is the power of a well-timed question.

One of the most gut-socking questions of all time came out of the mouth of Dean Rusk, the Secretary of State during President Lyndon Johnson's administration.

It seems that Charles de Gaulle, then the French President, was upset with the United States about something, so de Gaulle decided he'd retaliate. In a meeting with Rusk, he ordered him to have all United States military personnel out of France. The welcome mat was gone.

"Does your order include our dead soldiers?" Rusk asked quietly.

De Gaulle caught the meaning behind Rusk's question and was flummoxed. Tens of thousands of American soldiers had died on French soil.

Embarrassed, De Gaulle stood up and stalked out of the room. The order was never enforced.

Rusk could have demanded or pleaded that Americans not be required to leave, but instead posed his request in another, less challenging form.

Such is the power of a well-thought-out question.

THE WISDOM:

Those who don't ask questions think they know it

all. Those who do ask questions are sure they don't.

PART FOUR

The Wisdom We're (Still) Learning from This Pandemic

COVID-19 will be a defining moment in the 21st century. Our world will never be the same again.

ABOUT THE VIRUS.
YES, THAT VIRUS

"Not since World War II has all of humanity around the globe turned their attention towards a shared conflict."—UNKNOWN

BE PATIENT AS YOU READ THE following four chapters, remembering that the observations and opinions are not those of a doctor, scientist, expert, or someone privy to any more COVID-19 information than has been available to you. I'm just one of the 330 million American citizens, I could be your insurance agent, your mailman, or the dude you used to see (pre-Pandemic) snacking on samples at Costco. Despite my lack of credentials, I have observations and opinions about what has happened in the deadly days between March and December of 2020, that period of time that has resulted in our nation's most godawful year since 1941.

A lot of people smarter than me have screwed up their lives by making reckless choices related to this pandemic. Sadly, as I write this, many of those people will not be around to be part of 2021, the year of recovery.

Each of the following four chapters were written on the date indicated at the beginning of the chapter. Thus the thoughts and feelings were "back then", within that time frame, as we all watched history unfold. In retrospect, some of those observations were spot on, others were spot off. See for yourself.

Compare my observations to what you were thinking at that time. You surely must remember.

How could you forget?

—

This Chapter was written on July 1, 2020.

In November of 2019 Mary and I had just sold our Bend home and were now fulltime residents of Oro Valley Arizona, a suburb of Tucson. We'd barely unpacked our bags when suddenly we were smack dab in the early stages of the COVID-19 pandemic. We held our breaths along with the rest of the world as we watched China, Italy, NYC, and the state of Washington unravel, realizing that this pandemic would soon be on our own doorstep. The deaths were piling up; the search for testing and a vaccine had just begun. The world's finest scientists were burying their nose in the lab; all the rest of us could do was to mask up and stay at home.

This pandemic will be a race to the finish line, except that the finish line keeps moving, feinting one way, heading another. The data have been accumulating but hasn't yet been compiled. The world is confused, not even the experts know when or how this will end. If we aren't frightened, we should be.

In the meantime, all kinds of lifestyle-altering changes are appearing on the horizon. Take travel, for instance. A couple of decades ago we had to get used to surrendering our shoes, belt, and wristwatch to well-meaning government employees in blue uniforms. Now, we have to sanitize them before we put them back on.

A few weeks before the pandemic had been officially declared by the World Health Organization (March 11, 2020), I needed to fly from Tucson to Bend. Mary crammed my backpack with all the stuff she deemed necessary to survive the flight. In addition to wipes, sanitizers, and a mask, she included a snack so I wouldn't have to touch the potentially tainted stuff the airport shops sell or that the airline provides. She also included a book so I wouldn't have to purchase a magazine off the shelf or thumb through the airline magazine in the backseat pocket. My backpack overfloweth.

That trip would be the last 2020 travel experience in our house, via air anyway.

Small wonder, it's frightening out there.When we absolutely, positively have to leave the house, we could be rubbing shoulders with people who might be our unwitting killers, including our spouses, parents, kids, and the cashier at our neighborhood grocery store. The believers among us are staying at home, logging on to Amazon during the day, watching Netflix at night.

Home cooking is the newfound rage—a trend replicated in our house.Both Mary and I are long time careerists and cooking in any shape or form has never been our strong suit. Prior to COVID-19, we'd become accustomed to eating out three or four times a week. Now maybe we order takeout once a week, otherwise, it's recipes, some old, some new, some from friends, some from the internet.

Who among us hasn't cancelled at least one trip? Weddings, funerals, special events, conferences—you name it and we won't be going to it because it won't be happening. Well, at least this year... and in some cases, probably forever. The airlines are in for a long ride. Don't buy their stock.

Several days following the pandemic's official declaration— thanks to an early morning time that Safeway had set aside for us old folks—Mary and I went grocery shopping. That experience would not be a lifetime highlight. Grim-faced hoarders roamed the aisles, their carts stuffed with loaves of bread, packages of hamburger, and cans of soup—but not with toilet paper. Those shelves had already been picked clean.

After rounding up our grocery list, we looked on as the woman in front of us in the checkout line bought eight packages of frozen peas. Frozen peas? Who hoards frozen peas? I can understand ice cream, potato chips, or beer, but frozen peas? Crazy times, these.

The mood in Safeway that day was somber, bordering on fearful, each shopper worried that she wasn't going to get her fair share of the good stuff. In lieu of the muted sounds of friendly chatter that usually permeate the store, the only sounds were the wheels of grocery carts rolling up and down the aisles and the latest announcement that potatoes were now available in the produce section. The silence was deafening.

This is the fifth time in the last hundred years that a catastrophic event will change the lifestyle of Americans. This one is shaping up to be a doozy.

The first major lifestyle-changing event, in my lifetime anyway, was the Great Depression, Mom and Dad suffered through that one. I was born in 1936 and absorbed the lessons they learned from those days as I was growing up. Among other things, I learned the value of hard work and how to squeeze the bejesus out of a penny. Those lessons still endure, with me and with many people of my generation.

The second major life-changer was World War II. I can still remember bits and pieces of it, especially the VE Day neighborhood parade in 1945. I was nine and rode my two-wheeler—decked out in red, white, and blue—around the block with my parents looking happily on. The mood was giddy yet sobering. Victory had come at a horrible price.

Fifty-six years later, the third life-changer took place as we watched 9/11 unfold in real time. Travel paid the price that time too, and paranoia became the national mood. Homeland Security and the TSA were foisted upon us, quickly turning into the new normal.

Then there was the Great Recession in 2008. We brought this one on ourselves, with greed as the culprit. The Wall Street crowd got caught with their hands in our pockets. Who are those people who can influence our lives with a few keystrokes on a computer? Why don't they get real jobs: make something, help someone, do something constructive?

And now there's COVID-19, the Killer Pandemic. It's July of 2020 and we're in the frightening stage of what for sure will become a once-in-a-lifetime catastrophic event. What will the new normal be when this is over? Will we be attending concerts again? Football games with fans in the stands? Trade shows? Disneyland? Movies in theatres? There's a whole bunch of new normals roiling on the world's horizon. Tomorrow will not be the same as yesterday.

The pace of catastrophes seems to be accelerating. It's been a mere 20 years since the 21st century woke up on the wrong side of the bed. First there was 9/11, then the Great Recession, and now the pandemic, all in two short decades. Let's hope this isn't a harbinger of things to come for the rest of the century.

Three national disasters in 20 years? Is it just a coincidence or is there something more sinister going on? Is the world moving too fast for its denizens? Do we need to slow things down? In our unrelenting quest for the latest technology, are we leaving humanity behind? Or are the world's leaders the wrong people for their jobs?

And what about the hundreds of thousands of Americans who will have died before this pandemic has run its course? Behind each of those deaths will be a story. Oftentimes, that story will have included a poor decision—by a nursing home manager or a grandparent anxious to cuddle her grandkids or maybe by one of us attending a birthday party without wearing a mask.

One bad decision. That's all that it takes. Just one.

This pandemic will ultimately pass, just as all our national disasters have done. Five years from now the new normal will be in full swing and those of us who are still around will be busy living with it, and in it. Whatever *it* looks like.

In some cases, *it*—post-COVID-19's new normal—will be an improvement over what the old normal was. In other cases, hang on to your hat, especially if you're one of those people who don't enjoy change.

For now, however, buckle up and hunker down. There's a price that needs to be paid before this catastrophe passes. Let that price not be you. Or me.

THE WISDOM:

We're all in the same storm but not in the same boat."

OUT OF NOWHERE, ZOOM ZOOMED INTO MY LIFE

*"That's a very powerful message for the country—
if two 80-year-old men can successfully log into a
Zoom meeting, anything is possible."*
—JIMMY FALLON AFTER BERNIE SANDERS
ENDORSED JOE BIDEN ON ZOOM.

This Chapter was written on July 15, 2020.

WHAT CHANGED THE MOST FOR YOU during those early months of the coronavirus quarantining? What unintended consequences resulted when you became a prisoner in your own home? What weird stories happened to you as those mind-bending days dragged on?

We all had, or at least we all heard of, a weird story or two. Here's one that went viral:

Carolyn West is a tax accountant in Philadelphia. Once Zoom became a major part of her life, Carolyn, similar to the rest of us, suddenly started seeing herself as others see her. Thanks to looking at herself in a Zoom window, she decided her appearance needed an upgrade.

She'd never considered getting a lip injection before but considered it now. And then she did it. "It's because I have to look at my lips on Zoom all day," Carolyn said, as if the reason was obvious.

My own weird experience wasn't that dramatic, but it began when we moved from Oregon to Arizona. I'd been deeply involved in my community over the twenty-five years we'd lived in Bend, volunteering for a wide variety of projects and programs.

Suddenly, at age 83 and in our new adopted state, my community involvement came to a screeching halt. I began to lose touch with my Bend connections, co-volunteers, and friends. I was Tribeless in Tucson, my phone didn't ring, my texts didn't ping, and my emails quit buzzing. Overnight, I went from a half dozen meetings a day to none.

With little fanfare, I'd taken a giant step to becoming what many aging people fear more than anything else: irrelevant. I'm definitely one of those who fear it.

Then, as quarantining set in, I was introduced to Zoom, a user-friendly communication platform designed for technology challenged people like me. Quickly, I was able to restart my mentoring sessions, reboot my project-related meetings, and return to attending several monthly and quarterly board meetings. Thanks to Zoom I regained a measure of relevance and my spirits soared. My life was semi-back-to-normal again, sans handshakes and hugs.

Almost overnight, Zoom had become a staple in my life. Suddenly I went from being uninvolved to being busy, all for fifteen bucks a month. While that may not be as weird a story as having a lip injection, for me it has been life changing. Thank you for that, Zoom.

I'm not the only one that Zoom has impacted. In 2019 Zoom was averaging ten million users a day, by July of 2020, thanks to the pandemic, Zoom was averaging over 200 million participants every day. Like Kleenex, Post-Its, or Google, Zoom went from being a brand to a generic word in a short period of time. I was reminded of what happened with the fax back in the mid-1980s, when it went from being nowhere to everywhere in a few short months.

Zoom was not just for business-related meetings around our house. Mary is a member of two women's social groups, one in Bend and one here in Tucson; those women are her tribe. Each group includes eight women, enough to make up—surprise,

surprise—two golf foursomes. Those two groups, social in nature, also discovered the relative ease of Zoom. Suddenly, our living room was filled with the sounds of giggling and laughter again, all thanks to Zoom.

The best thing about Zoom? It's geezer-friendly, meaning it's quick and easy and requires little geekiness. All that's needed is a digital device with a camera, which most iPads have. Like the majority of people my age, I'm a digital dope; I don't Skype, tweet, or have an Instagram page. If I can Zoom, so can most other doddering duffers. It's Technology for Dummies.

A side benefit of Zooming is that you don't have to dress up for meetings. Well, at least from the waist down. Shorts, warmups, pajamas, underwear, anything goes—below the belt, that is. OK, so you do have to wear a shirt or a blouse. In a related announcement, Walmart reported that in March of 2020 they suddenly began selling inordinately more shirts than pants, more tops than bottoms. Herd behavior at work.

And that's not all that makes Zoom easier. We don't have to brush our teeth or take a breath mint before a meeting. Just comb our hair, pull on a clean top, and log on.

Here's one final reason why Zoom is so cool for the people who use it. We don't have to get in the car or catch a plane to get where we're going. Just click on the link and we can Zoom from our bedroom or kitchen with our fellow Zoomees who are in Singapore or London.

We can Zoom from our bathroom too, I suppose.

Zoom has evolved into the ultimate social distancing tool. It, or something akin to it, will be part of our life long after COVID-19 has disappeared.

THE WISDOM:

9am meeting in NYC, 10am meeting in LA. All in

two hours and no need for TSA.

SEVEN MONTHS LATER: STILL MORE ABOUT THAT VIRUS

"Today's weather: Room temperature."—ANONYMOUS

This Chapter was written on October 15, 2020:

IT'S BEEN SEVEN MONTHS NOW SINCE this pandemic was officially declared. Quarantine fatigue has set in, we miss our social interactions, we miss going to a movie, we're tired of spending our days within our own four walls. I can't help but think about those friends of ours who have kids at home, they've gotta be going nuts. Their kids have gotta be going nuts too. No winners here.

In addition to the frustration of being confined, we are ordered to do so, which smacks of Big Brothership to some. We're sick and tired of masks, sanitizers, and being ruled by the needs of the herd. We're tired of being dictated to, we want our freedom back.

Now don't get me wrong, I'm not saying I disagree with the sacrifices we've directed to make as we wade further and further into the COVID-19 abyss. I'm just saying this pandemic life is getting old and tiresome. We're ready for some semblance of the old days again.

So there, I hope you'll excuse me. Just needed to whine.

Now I feel better.

In truth, I feel guilty about whining. Unlike millions of other folks, I don't have to worry about my kids climbing the wall, or struggle with remote learning, or being unable to interact with their friends. I can't imagine dealing with all of that parenting stuff while struggling to make a living at the same time. Remote working helps, but still...

There are times, I guess, and this is one of them, when being old can be a good thing. Heck, I was already accustomed to being around the house during the day when the coronavirus came along, this is nothing new. Quarantining has been an inconvenience, but it hasn't been a sentence. There's seven billion people worse off than me.

In truth, I have it easy. I play golf, I write, and I do Pilates, the same things I'd be doing whether or not COVID-19 was going on. My days aren't *that* much different from what they used to be, except that I don't have to drive to get where I do what I do. Thanks again, Zoom, for that.

But still, a movie in a theater with buttered popcorn would be nice. Or an outdoor concert with music and mingling. Or a beer after golf with friends.

I'm setting a bad example here, I know, I need to stop complaining. It's just that pessimism seems to be the national mood right now. I get it, we're at war here and it's a war we're losing, more than 200,000 Americans have died, and there's no end in sight. Millions of workers have lost their jobs and our President is recovering in the hospital rather than being at his desk in the White House.

When this latest national disaster has finally run its course, COVID-19 will rank as the number two lifestyle-changing catastrophic event that has unfolded in my lifetime, and it may well take over the top spot if the vaccine doesn't come along soon. If the criteria were fatalities, World War II would currently claim the number one spot, but the pandemic is a long way from being over. I'm not making any bets.

No one knows how this pandemic is going to stack up against our country's previous catastrophes, but here are some statistics to consider:

- COVID-19 stands hauntingly on the threshold of being the number-one ranked catastrophe in terms of dollars cost. World War II cost the U.S. $3 trillion in today's dollars. Last I heard, COVID-19 was at $3 trillion and counting. The coronavirus is a cinch to "win" this one.

- Slightly over 400,000 American soldiers died in World War II. As things stand today, COVID-19 has claimed more than 200,000 American lives, so I wouldn't count it out.(2,977 people died on 9/11, so as shocking as that tragedy was, the cost in lives was miniscule). Granted, those 400,000 World War II lives lost were mostly young men while the average age of COVID-19's deaths is significantly older. But still…

- Twenty-six million jobs disappeared in the first five weeks following the pandemic declaration, which means we lost 11 years of job growth in less than two months. How could anyone dream up a scenario like that? (WWII actually *created* jobs. Go figure.)

Then there's the toll on America's businesses, of both the small business and Fortune 500 variety (with certain niches excepted, mostly in the technology sector). Tens of thousands of American small businesses have closed their doors, never to reopen again, due to no fault of their own. Key industries such as hospitality, travel, and entertainment are either being disrupted or are disappearing.

And finally, there's us. Our nation's fractured, divisive, and often confused American citizens. Citizens who aren't sure who to believe when it comes to the seriousness of this virus. In an infamous incident that took place in San Antonio recently, a 30-old patient died after attending a—I'm not making this up—a COVID-19 party. "I think I made a mistake" were the man's final words. "I thought COVID-19 was a hoax."

A COVID-19 party? C'mon man, how can that be?

But I sort of understand what was behind that man's confusion. After all, we're all wondering, these days, who can we believe? Do the facts and figures we're hearing come from a nonpartisan source? Who can we trust to tell us the truth?

Where's Walter Cronkite when we need him?

As always happens when change takes place too fast, there are unintended consequences, some good and some not so good. The not-so-good are still up in the air, but the good, in this aging codger's life anyway, include:

- I lost ten pounds the first month following the pandemic declaration without even trying. Previous to COVID-19, we ate more than 50% of our meals in restaurants; today we eat 100% of them at home. As a result of the smaller portions, we're eating less.
- Our family's monthly expenses plummeted to almost half of what they were pre-COVID-19. Transportation, eating out, entertainment, and travel were the biggest losers, but just about everything decreased. Well, except for Amazon.
- Our dogs are loving this quarantining routine. Petting is reliably available and Bogey and Rudy are hoping the new normal will keep things this way.

Similar to the majority of Americans, I'm a social creature, so what I miss most are handshakes and hugs. Even a touch on the arm, a pat on the back, or a peck on the cheek will do. I still find myself reaching out to touch someone, then drawing my hand back in midflight. I'm hoping that whatever the new normal turns out to be, these old and traditional expressions of caring and concern will make the cut.

I also miss being around people, I'm an unapologetic observer of them in all their fascinating forms. I love to pick out attendees at a concert, a sports event, or a business gathering, and observe their facial expressions, their body language, their way of communicating.

Even airports are fun. Such pickings have been slim of late; I've had to depend on YouTube, Facebook and LinkedIn to get my people fix. Those platforms are better than nothing, but a long way from what I'm used to.

Meanwhile, Mary and I are playing by the rules, always wearing a mask, maintaining our distance, keeping our hands washed and our fingers crossed. All of which, with the exception of the mask, is not *that* much different from what we were doing before the coronavirus came along.

Except that now there's a gun at our back.

THE WISDOM:

Wrenching change can be painful, but with it

comes the opportunity for wrenching progress.

WHAT WILL POST-VIRUS LIFE LOOK LIKE?

"I think we can all agree that in 2015 not a single person got the answer correct to the question 'Where do you see yourself five years from now?'"—UNKNOWN

This Chapter was written on December 31, 2020.

DECEMBER IS FINALLY WINDING DOWN IN this uber-cruel year of 2020. The virus is surging again, our hospitals are bursting at the seams. Our caregivers—God love 'em—are running on empty; the degree of suffering they must be witnessing is unimaginable. Heroes arise from the ashes of tragedy, thankfully our American caregivers fill that role.

Proving once more that necessity is the mother of invention, the U.S. got its scientific and pharmaceutical act together and the vaccine has arrived, ahead of schedule. But, in the same breath, the CDC estimates that anywhere from 20% to 40% of Americans will choose not to vaccinate.

How can that be? 20% to 40% of our citizens are anti-vaxxers? Whose fault is that? Theirs or someone else's?

The answer is, it's someone else's. Simply put, that 20% to 40% doesn't trust our leaders to properly advise them when making major decisions. I recently spoke with a friend in Canada who said they don't have an anti-vaxxer subset of people up there. Everyone masks in Canada and everyone will choose to vaccinate, he assures me. Why the difference, it makes me wonder?

I recently saw an estimate of where I sit on the vaccination priority chart. The CDC is recommending that round one will go, as it should, to health care workers and long-term care facility residents. Round two will include—yay!—those of us who are over 75; which puts me in the same tranche as grocery store workers and prison guards. I feel a tad guilty about such an elevated status; there's a lot of skilled and caring people out there who have contributed more than I have to get us through this. All I've done is grow old.

Now that we have some assurance of the "how" and "when" that COVID-19 will be over, what about the "what?" What will the new normal look like, post pandemic? What in our lives, is going to change?

Ask a dozen people that question, and you'll get a dozen different answers. Here's one person's answer that I read a while back:

Rose Marcario, Patagonia's upbeat CEO, wrote, 'Right now we're writing history and we can choose a better world. We can create a new world that values caregiving and the planet. It's our choice to make.'

Rose, the CEO of one of the world's most thoughtful and caring brands, went on to opine that simply reopening our country shouldn't be enough. She wants to remake it. Before we can do that, she says, we must first reimagine what we want to be and what we want to look like. Then we can figure out how to get there.

More power to Rose and her well-intentioned musings, I think most of us would agree with what she said. Our country *could* use some remaking.

However, if Rose were to ask, I'd suggest that someday will be the right time for that remake to come to pass, but that someday is not now. For now, Rose will have to file her suggestion in the "to be considered later" folder. Later, after we've digested, adjusted, and adopted what has just happened to us, then maybe we can begin thinking about Rose's vision.

But first, we need to identify and adjust to the new normal that will surely evolve from the aftermath of COVID-19. That evolution will be especially impactful within the two environments in which we Americans spend the majority of our time: at home and at work.

Thanks to spending an inordinate amount of our time at home the past nine months, many of us have upgraded both the technology and the comfort of where we live. We can now work more productively there, while being more relaxed too. Also, our commute has been drastically shortened, thanks to our office being just down the hall from our bedroom.

Today, following a day of working remotely at home, we can now order in a better meal than most of us could prepare ourselves. Following which we can be entertained by the latest offerings of Netflix, Hulu, Disney, or any one of the 14-and-growing video streaming services available. How did all those businesses know that COVID-19 was coming? What did they know that the rest of us didn't?

Our home is now our castle. It is also our entertainment center. Sure, we still need a car to take the kids to soccer practice and shop at Costco, but to a much larger degree than pre-pandemic, the family car has been relegated to spending more time in the garage.

Then there's our workplace. Many businesses will have, if they haven't already, either evolved to fulltime remote working or, more likely, will have adopted some sort of a home-and-away hybrid model. By so doing, those businesses can conserve on office space, while their employees can cut back on, or eliminate, the burden of commuting. Everyone wins—except, that is, the people who own the half-empty office buildings.

Meanwhile, wouldn't you know it, there's software being developed that will measure the productivity of remote workers. Intrusive? Sure, but there's a tradeoff, we won't have the boss breathing down our necks anymore. Now our success will be measured by the quantity and quality of our work. Sure sounds like a fair trade to me.

Our consuming habits are changing too. Since the pandemic began, many of us are consuming significantly less than we were pre-virus and are banking or investing the difference. We've cut back on activities such as travel, entertainment, and eating out. While we miss the diversion that comes from leaving the house and going out on the town, it feels good to be spending less and saving more. This proclivity to cut back on our spending won't last forever, of course, but there's a part of us that says that spending less is a good thing.

As other new normals evolve, that won't mean out with all the old and in with all the new. Some of the old will remain, like the need for family and friends and social interactions. Man is a social creature; the new normal won't be changing that.

But there's plenty of the old normal on the endangered list. Here's a smattering of those that are rife for change:

- **Shopping**: COVID-19 has given an additional boost to online shopping, which means that our local businesses are paying the price. As if they weren't already.
- **Malls:** Been to a mall lately? Neither have I. So much infrastructure, so few people.
- **Higher Education:** The pandemic has hastened the rise of digital learning at the expense of brick-and-mortar schools. Sadly, higher ed has, for the average American anyway, priced itself out of the market.
- **K-12 Education:** The classroom will be back. Kids need kids. And real-live teachers too.
- **Technology:** Computer sales are booming, which means more people are online. Which is not always a good thing.
- **Transportation:** Time spent in a car is usually wasted time. People are finding ways to drive less, which is good for the environment as well as for the pocketbook. But not so good for Chevron, Saudi Arabia, or Texas.
- **Remote Working:** People need people, but we also enjoy working in our PJs and being close to the kids and the fridge.
- **Entertainment:** We old folks may still head for a theatre now and then, but today's young'uns can entertain themselves at home.

- **Eating Out:** The best restaurants will survive, the weakest ones won't: It's Economics 101 at work. Most likely, the industry was overbuilt when the pandemic began.
- **Business Travel:** Zoom saves time and money. Businesses can use more of both.
- **Tourism:** Short term, bleak. Long term, bright. Young people still value experiences over stuff.
- **Pets:** During the pandemic, pet adoptions have surged. Looking for a growth industry?

Here's hoping that whatever the new normal has in store for us, it won't mean that attending events will go the way of the BlackBerry. And here's hoping that it doesn't mean that Skype and Zoom will replace sharing lunch with a colleague or beer with a friend. And finally, here's hoping that it doesn't mean touching elbows or bumping fists will replace handshakes and hugs.

I know that, in the end, when COVID-19 finally becomes yesterday's news, there will be no mistaking tomorrow for yesterday. The future never looks like the past, and the new normal won't be anything like the old normal. Change is usually for the better, the only problem is that change is happening too fast.

I also know that, a year from now, most of the world will be maskless and back to some sense of normality again. That's the way disruptions work and today, Christmas of 2020, we're at the peak of COVID-19's disrupting. I've lived through disruptions before. The pain always comes before the privilege.

And I will, I really will, welcome a lot of the change that is sure to result. But I'm also an old guy and there will be parts of my life I want back again. I've been waiting patiently to see my grandkids, to sit in the stands at a basketball game, or hunker down at the bar in my favorite pub and BS with the bartender.

But I'll be fascinated to see what the new normal will include, if I can hang around that long. Change is good, no matter how old we are when it happens.

It all happened so fast, it seems. In February the sky was blue; by the end of March, it had turned black. On this final day in December, it is even blacker.

But someday the blue sky will return. It will be a different shade of blue perhaps, but with a little luck and a lot of ingenuity, it could be a fresher and more inviting shade.

And a brighter one, too.

THE WISDOM:

This too shall pass…thanks to science and our

government's deep pockets.

WHY WISDOM COMES WITH AGE

"As the body diminishes, the soul gets richer."
—JOHN O'DONOHUE

WE ALL HAVE OUR EARLY MORNING routines. Mine is infinitely more complicated today than it was thirty years ago. I now wake up, stretch, take a few deep breaths, and then make a rash of grunting and groaning noises. Next, I inventory all my moving parts, making sure they're still working. The majority of them have been, up to now.

Then I slide out of bed and shuffle off to the kitchen for my first glass of water. It's tough to stay hydrated when you live in Arizona, especially when you don't like the taste of the tap water here. If we can put a man on the moon why can't we make water that tastes like, say, Pepsi? That shouldn't be asking too much.

Water in hand, I then shuffle off to the desk in my office, which is right around the corner from the kitchen. As I sit down, I ask myself the same question I've been asking myself for the last thirty years: "How much money do I feel like today?"

Fifty years ago, when I'd ask myself this question, I'd pound my chest, and say to myself, "I feel like a million bucks today!" Then I'd brush my teeth before heading out to run a four-minute mile or hit sixty home runs or do whatever the entrepreneurial equivalent of those feats happened to be.

Sure, there were times when I felt more like $750,000 in the morning than a million bucks. Or even $500,000, if it was the day after someone's bachelor party.

Today, I'm 84. I still wake up in the morning—always a good start—but most days I feel like somewhere around ten thousand bucks, which is a long way away from the million dollars of fifty years ago. As the day progresses and my body oils up, I can get that number up to, say, $100,000. Or if it's a warm, sunny day in the springtime and the robins are chirping and the tulips blooming, maybe I can stretch it to a couple hundred thousand. But that's about as good as it gets these days. Age has taken its toll, on the body anyway.

I'll admit that this is not exactly a ringing endorsement for getting old. But let's face it: There's a price we pay for everything and we're paying now for all those crazy-ass things we did when we were younger. What goes around, comes around, they say, and old age is come-around time.

While my body may be depreciating at a rapid clip, I'm happy to report that my mind is not. There are some days when, if all my synapses are firing, my mind can feel like at least a half a million bucks. Sure, it isn't as quick as it used to be, but given time, it can still come to the right conclusion.

The reason for the difference between my physical and mental state is, in part, that I've taken better care of my mind than I have my body. I'm not saying I'm as smart or have as good a memory as I did 50 years ago; you wouldn't want me on your debate team. But what I can do much better today than I could in the old days is to Connect the Dots and See the Big Picture.

While those two capabilities don't make me any smarter, they do make me wiser, which means I'm better able to help those who can use my rusty but trusty brand of wisdom. Wise is a good thing to be at any age, and for me it seems to be peaking right about now.

It's nice to have something peak when you get to be this age.

The *Free Dictionary* defines the term "connecting the dots" as "understanding something by piecing together hints or other bits of information." This definition describes the ability we old timers have of being able to visualize the details (i.e., the dots) that make up a problem and then, thanks to the intuition we've earned over decades of experiences, connect those dots and weave them into a meaningful solution. We may not have a full grasp of the details themselves, but we've read this book before and we know how it ends.

The *Free Dictionary* then goes on to define "the big picture" as "the general, overall, or long-term scheme of something, as opposed to the specific details or present preoccupations." The Big Picture is, the dictionary is saying, what we see once our mind has connected all the dots and reconciled them with our stash of past experiences. The dots then, are the brew, the big picture is the stew.

Such is the miracle of aging. Somehow, we just seem to know the solution, even when we didn't know we knew it when the question was asked.

In the end, for those of us who have experienced an active life and have earned our wisdom the hard way, there is an inexhaustible supply of people out there who could use what we've learned. Most are young and currently in our network: our kids, our grandkids, our relative's kids, our friend's kids, our neighbor's kids, our church's kids. Kids who would welcome an opportunity to learn even a smattering of what we've picked up over the years.

These are the kids who will be tomorrow's change makers and world shapers. They are our future politicians, teachers, and clergy. They are the kids setting out on the road we've already traveled.

Why shouldn't we share what we've learned? There's no downside, but plenty of upsides.

For them and for us.

THE WISDOM:

If a tree falls in the forest and no one hears it, does

it make a sound? If a man is wise and doesn't

share it, does his wisdom make a difference?

IN DEATH WE COME TOGETHER

"Honor Thy Family—the one you were born with, the one you've acquired during your lifetime and the Family of Man."—MARILYN STASIO

I INTENDED FOR THE PRECEDING CHAPTER to be the last one in this book. But life got in the way...

—

My son Mike passed away from cancer on September 15, 2020 in Portland, Oregon. He was 54.

That's not the way life is supposed to happen. Mike was supposed to mourn his mother and me when our time came, not the other way around. A child's passing is life's cruelest twist of fate for a parent. No words can describe how it feels.

Mike was the youngest of my three sons, with Jim Jr. the oldest and Todd bringing up the middle. All three have been the kind of kids that make a parent proud. They've been caring adults and contributing citizens. What more can a father ask?

It's one month following Mike's death as I write this, his passing is still too raw to pass on the details. Besides, they aren't important. What is important are the lessons our family learned from the life he led and how we'll be making those lessons part of our lives. Mike would be pissed if something positive didn't come from this.

While death by cancer is uncompromising, Mike spit in its face right up 'til the end. He died in the early morning in his own bedroom with Cydney, the Queen of All Girlfriends, and Jim, the Saint of all Oldest Brothers, at his bedside. The rest of our family—at least those of us who were able to travel while COVID-19 was raging—were lodged in a rented home nearby. We were at Mike's side for the week leading up to his death, sharing laughs, retelling stories, and saying goodbye.

It was 6:12 on a Tuesday morning when he took his last breath.

Today, surprisingly, amidst the sadness and grieving, I feel no bitterness or anger for a life ended too soon. I say this in part because there's no one to blame and in part because there's no benefit that comes from those two emotions. Besides, Mike wouldn't want us wasting our time doing something that wasn't upbeat and positive.

Our family learned so much as we met his Portland friends who shared in his boisterous and adventurous life. We laughed and we cried as the sometimes sidesplitting, often frightening, and always entertaining Mike stories piled up. A strange dynamic ensued and somehow, the more we heard, the more grateful we became that he was our son and brother.

In death, Mike left his family a legacy. And legacies are the greatest gift of them all.

The primary lesson he taught us was to be true to oneself. Be who you are and make no excuses for it. He joyfully called himself the black sheep of our family, but he was wrong. There was nothing black or dark about him. Rather, he was a purple sheep: extraordinary, unique, and vastly different, a man who reveled in his freedom and independence. He loved the unpredictability and the adrenalin rush that came from never knowing what was around the corner. Every day was unique. Every day a surprise.

A tattoo on the inside of his left forearm said "NOW" and served as a constant reminder (as if he needed it) to live in the present, which is exactly what he did. Planning and preparation were not part of his life. If he felt like doing something, he up and did it. Now, with no explanation required.

Mike also taught us about passion and dedication. He was a fly fisherman extraordinaire; the uglier the weather, the more likely it was that he and his dog Ike (or later, Halo) would jump in his truck and make tracks for his favorite Oregon river or stream. His quarry was almost always the elusive steelhead, the fish of a thousand casts, because that's what it usually takes to catch one. When he'd reel a steelie in, he'd relish the moment by holding the exhausted fish in his hands before gingerly releasing it to fight again.

He was, in effect, a 54-year-old millennial, which meant he worked to live, unlike me and my generation who lived to work. He called himself a carpenter, but he was so much more than that. He was a gifted builder and a trusted designer, much of his work exhibited a functional, yet rich and creative flair.

When Mike first called the family with the news of his terminal diagnosis, his older brother Jim, recently widowed in yet another 2020 Schell family tragedy, packed his bags in Minneapolis, drove to Portland, and for the four months leading up to Mike's death, settled in as his roommate, friend, brother, and caregiver. Until the end, Jim and Cydney were with him 24/7, a constant reminder that love is the greatest caregiver of them all.

We'll all grieve and tell Mike stories again in Portland on June 3, 2021, the day that would have been his 55th birthday. Cydney is planning a Celebration of Mike's Life on that day, a celebration that will include depositing his ashes in one of his favorite Oregon rivers in the company of family and friends. A Schell reunion will follow, the first in the history of our family.

So thank you, Mike, for tightening the bond between those of us who loved you. And thank you for nurturing a colorful and inspiring life and for sharing it with your family and your friends. And finally, thank you for the free-spirited, live-for-the-moment wisdom you wove into the tapestry of all our lives.

You, little brother, are an inspiration to us all.

I debated about including Mike's story in this book, especially as the final chapter. The last thing an author wants to do is to end his book on a downer.

Except that...

...Mike's life and the story behind it aren't downers. Certainly, his passing was heartbreaking to those of us who loved him, but his life was full and rich and inspirational. He motivated us to be our own best selves. To be more like him.

As a result, Mike's story and his life have been uplifting for our family. We hope he can inspire you as well.

RIP Mike Schell
1966–2020
He gave so much more than he took.

THE WISDOM:

There are those whose light burns so brightly that

their shadows still flicker long after they're gone.

At peace, for once. Mike, Todd and Jim

In a rare passive mood. The toothpick helps.

The look on his face says it all.